GOD'S PLAN
FOR THE USA

7 *BIBLE TRUTHS* ARE THE ONLY WAY TO *SAVE AMERICA*

STEVEN ANDREW

ACTS ONE EIGHT
Publishing

GOD'S PLAN FOR THE USA

7 BIBLE TRUTHS ARE THE ONLY WAY TO SAVE AMERICA

STEVEN ANDREW

ISBN 9780977955091
Revised November 2016

Copyright © 2015 by Steven Andrew
Published by ACTS ONE EIGHT Publishing™
ActsOneEightPublishing.com

*Also available as hardcover: ISBN 9780977955053
and eBook: ISBN 9780977955060*

Scripture quotations are from the King James Version of the Holy Bible and are marked "KJV". References to God are capitalized. Brackets in verses or quotations are by the author for use as clarification. Other Scriptures are from the TrueKJV™ Holy Bible.

References given in this book do not constitute an endorsement. This book provides information to readers. It is sold and/or provided with the understanding that the publisher and author are not engaged to render any type of legal advice. Your actions are your responsibility. The book may be updated from time to time. Web sites and information listed in this book may change.

Contents

Patriotism

Preface

Honestly, growing up I would not have imagined writing a book that provides God's answers to save the USA. Like many people, I am concerned for the well-being of our nation and our future. That is why I devoted myself to prayer and searching the Bible and American history to find God's plan to save our country.

As far as I remember, I have believed there was something unique that makes the USA stand out above others. I have always loved America. As a teenager, I prayed to receive Jesus Christ and He instantly changed my life. By loving God and country, I saw God raise me up to speak His message of hope, helping millions of lives with the Gospel of Jesus Christ.

This book provides God's roadmap for our nation, while we discover His will. I believe that turning to Him with all of our heart and soul will heal our land. It is God's desire. He cares for us and wants us to be free of all our trouble—from economic collapse to terrorists. We can overcome spiritual darkness, families can be strong, and each of us can have peace and liberty!

Do you want God to bless your life? Follow His plan. Do you want God to bless the USA? Then as a nation we need to follow His plan. There are *7 Bible Truths* that guarantee God will save the USA and bless your life. I say "guaranteed" because when we turn to God, He blesses us.

In the few hours it takes to read this life-changing book, you will learn God's urgent message to the USA. Church groups should study a chapter a week together. I am looking for a minimum of *One Million Americans on the LORD's Side*™. If that is you, then sign up at my website. I believe that there are millions of faithful Americans—Christians and ministers!

God is good. Let's thank Him for His mercy and faithfulness, for He kindly offers forgiveness to us through His Son. Please join me in living *God's Plan for the USA*; we will not only get out of our national danger, but these *7 Bible Truths* are how we make the USA great again. Always remember, Jesus loves you.

Steven Andrew
USA Christian Church
www.USA.church

꽃

I am praying for you; I seek God for you to be strengthened in Jesus Christ. He created you with a special purpose, personally and for the USA. I am excited because soon you will discover the hope and joy that comes by being fully equipped to live God's plan. You will know God better, and He will be glorified in your life and in our Christian nation.

God has blessed me with exceptional people to review the manuscripts. I thank God for each person and I pray for God to strengthen each of you as well.

Introduction

The Crisis That Threatens the USA's Survival
... And Our Future

Our nation stands on the precipice of imminent disaster. Godlessness is ravaging the land and signs of the end are being seen, but the people carry on as though nothing is happening. Many eyes are closed as freedom and truth are stripped away. People spend their time pursuing popularity, feeding obsessions of power and wealth, and letting TV and social media sap away their moral compasses. The USA's foundation, even our very existence, is at stake while many are either oblivious or fight the wrong battles.

America is in a struggle against our greatest danger since 1776 when our founders fought for Christian liberty to freely follow God. Our nation's founding priority is Christian religious liberty, which is protected by the Constitution. There are many signs of this alarming crisis that call for each of us to live *God's Plan for the USA,* even above other priorities.

Faithful Americans are losing jobs, not being promoted, going to jail, and are fined for following the Word of God. Daily threats from the ungodly seek to discourage believers from obeying our consciences and refusing to be a part of activities against our beliefs.

Those who stand for the principles that God and our founders call us to follow are now labeled as "haters" and "bigots". As you may have heard, Christian florists, bakers, clerks, business owners, military members, and students are undergoing persecution for choosing to stand for what they believe.[1] Kim Davis, a county clerk in Kentucky, was jailed for obeying her belief to oppose same-sex marriage.[2]

Our nation's founders came to America to freely serve the LORD without persecution. But a war is being waged against Christianity and our true American beliefs by unfaithful politicians, government funded educators, court officials, military leaders, the media, misdirected businesses, and anti-God groups. Rather than following God, these anti-American forces are pursuing the removal of Christian beliefs and freedoms. This trend must be reversed immediately. When people stop following God as their top priority, the greatest troubles in life befall them (2 Chronicles 15:2).

Our other God-given rights are under attack. Threats against our nation's founding laws are becoming everyday experiences. For example, freedom of speech is being limited. There are places where we are told that the First Amendment doesn't apply. Instead of speaking their opinions freely, people are intimidated into silence. These restrictions are particularly targeting those who would express opinions contrary to homosexuality, tyranny, Islam, foreigners, and killing innocent children by abortion.

A quick search of the news will reveal that those opposing the LORD, such as ungodly politicians, gays, Muslims, and abortionists, are often given "special rights" that trample the God-given rights that our founders assured us. For example, the Supreme Court and Barack Obama persecute Christians but give special status to gays by the court opinion to stop the ban on same-sex marriage[3] that always existed. Even though Mike Huckabee explained that same-sex marriage "is not law" as the Supreme Court has no Constitutional authority to make laws,[4] many are deceived to think unconstitutional acts like this are legal. Congress makes laws; the president signs them.

The safety of our nation is at stake. Terrorists are crossing our open border. A news report found Homeland Security busing in and helping likely Muslim terrorists and then releasing them in the USA, which endangers our nation.[5] Many politicians favor illegal aliens over Americans. The whole nation, especially school children, the elderly, and the poorest among us are in jeopardy from these risks.

Without the Constitution and following its true meaning, the legal protection of our rights vanishes. This is seen by politicians who have pledged to uphold the Constitution, but scheme to destroy, replace, or update it. Likewise, lawlessness abounds by neglecting our personal responsibility to enforce the Constitution. Consequently, the USA becomes like other countries, having few or no rights for those who love God.

The financial problems are more serious than many realize with rumors of a great financial shaking.[6] People have less money and poverty levels are the highest they have ever been. Millions of Americans don't have jobs and forty percent of the unemployed have stopped looking for work.[7] Nearly fifty million are on food stamps and millions more use other types of food assistance.[8]

Our founders gave us a nation with no personal taxes, money backed by gold and silver, limits on federal spending, and representatives who serve the people. Today, it is common to pay more than half of our earnings in taxes, our currency is based on debt, and politicians betray the people for self-seeking or corporate interests. Less money remains to spend on basic needs like housing, clothing, and food.

The biggest national debt in history, printing currency without backing, and inflation are setting the stage for a financial catastrophe. Foreign currencies like the Chinese Yuan or others may replace the dollar as the world's standard form of currency.[9] Communist China, with godless leaders, owns a significant part of the USA debt.[10] Without intervention from God, people could lose much of their wealth in a financial correction or dollar devaluation.

While people believe in God, many often make Him second or third place in their lives and not enough speak-up or cry out to Him for our nation to follow His ways. Instead of God-given rights, some want "rights" to sin without being shamed for breaking God's laws, which results in destruction.

The government is taking steps to control everything and that means greater debt, more inefficiency, lower quality, and higher costs. Our privacy has been stolen, personal property has been converted to government property without due process, higher healthcare costs have been forced upon everyone, and schools have fallen to below the world average in math, lower than Vietnam.[11] The USA has become just average in reading, lower than Estonia and Chinese Taipai.[11]

Instead of having the freedom to do what we want with personal responsibility to God, we see the oppression by a police state with every action being watched, listened to, and judged. It is becoming more common for police to respond with military force against citizens. Non-military federal agencies have bought over two billion rounds of ammunition, raising concerns if it will be used against Americans.[12]

Jesus said, *every city or house divided against itself shall not stand* (Matthew 12:25). We see division as non-Christian forces pit Christians against each other, cause hatred between different races, political groups, and economic classes that has resulted in unrest, riots, and chaos.

Our children's lives are at risk. Will they know what it means to be a free American? Children went from learning the alphabet with Bible verses to shamefully being taught tolerance of false gods and pagan beliefs. Our public schools went from teaching to *love the Lord your God... is the first, the great, the indispensable duty of every rational being* and that *sin is the source of all evil,*[13] to censoring God and teaching evil ways. Children who do not know God make sinful citizens and are in danger of not going to Heaven. As a result, every parent should be concerned for their children.

Even though it is a historic communist enemy, China is training with our military inside the USA;[14] other foreign militaries with no allegiance to Americans have bases here.[15] Millions of foreigners are buying property and getting on welfare. Those without loyalty to the USA are unlikely to side with Americans in the event of an invasion or martial law. Our enemies are lining up, whether it is Iran, ISIS, China, North Korea, or other anti-God peoples. With our military persecuting Christians and having no shame of gay sin, how can God go out with our armies? (Psalm 60:10) These are signs our national security is at risk.

One of the biggest problems is that many don't know what the Bible says to do to save the USA from the crisis. People have been side-tracked to think that the troubles arise from the ideologies of Democrats or Republicans rather than national disobedience to God. Still others claim that we can do nothing to change the degradation from sin because "prophecies" foretell these times and look to "harbingers" or "blood moons" as prophetic signs, but have forgotten our priority to make disciples of our nation. Others think that political corruption and the New World Order are too big for God to remove.

It's time we change our course using timeless truths from God. The opportunity to fix this urgent problem is limited. We must act quickly in applying the Biblical solutions that will prevent the ruin of our nation. We must ask: What does Scripture say is happening? Does the Bible show that there is something more important that we must know and do?

With all of these problems that affect our lives greatly, God has a better way for us. In *God's Plan for the USA,* you will discover what happens when Americans follow seven remarkable *Bible Truths.* Applying these Bible promises immediately improves our lives *and* the condition of our nation. God promises that these truths from His Word will bring great blessings to us and save the USA from destruction—and even captivity as happened to Israel. Are you ready to learn God's plan?

1
Do You Want the USA to Follow God?

"Blessed is the nation whose God is the LORD..."
Psalm 33:12 KJV

A small group of faithful men, young and old, were united in silent submission to humbly seek God's deliverance and protection. They understood that His will was for our nation to freely follow Jesus Christ.

The decisions that our First Continental Congress made, based on the study of the Bible and prayer to our Christian God, would lead to events creating a document that would change the course of millions of lives centuries into the future, including yours.

The birth of the Declaration of Independence two years later, one of the most important documents in history, was derived from such acts of prayer. This simple, yet courageous show of loyalty to obey God instead of man would bring the greatest levels of Christian religious liberty ever seen, with unprecedented blessings to all who follow in agreement.

The first act of Congress - George Washington, John Adams, Samuel Adams, and our Founding Fathers praying in Jesus' name and reading the Holy Bible in 1774. Washington (center), John Adams (sixth from top left) and Samuel Adams (left of John Adams in light coat).

Our founders humbling themselves to seek God is the first act of Congress. Walking in covenant gave our founding fathers the bold confidence to petition Him for deliverance from oppression as they laid the foundations for self-government built on Jesus Christ and His Word. God answered the prayers of our faithful forefathers and blessed our nation with His liberty, abundance, and peace.

However, why can't we say that we are enjoying these same blessings today that the USA is known for—with our nation in such dire straits? Is there a way to still receive the good things that God wants to kindly give us?

The answer to have God's blessings is found in *7 Bible Truths.* They guarantee great blessings no matter how things may look, for His truth stands forever! God promises His favor both for the USA and our lives personally when we seek Him and follow His Word. Having God's favor is of greater value than everything else. But before we discover these powerful *Bible Truths,* let's understand how richly the LORD has blessed the USA and answer two questions that require our prompt attention, "Do you want the USA to follow God?" and "Is God judging our country?" Answering these questions is especially important because of their affect to our future.

Do You Want the USA to Obey God's Will?

Often to find meaning for our lives we pursue so many different things. We try to find meaning in our careers, relationships, our children, in material things, our toys, or our wealth and status. I did this earlier in my life with sports and business. But often we don't realize that God has placed us in this life for a greater purpose. He has a plan for us to fulfill. How well do we know His will for our lives and nation?

With the USA in a serious emergency, how many truly know God's answer of how we got here, or the extent of the crisis. In fact, many have been misled into believing that sinful policies and behaviors are actually good and that they are indicators of progress. Still others ignore the deterioration of our nation with no thought toward America's future.

As an inspiration to us, we know our founders pursued God's plan to freely serve Him and succeeded. To overcome persecution, they left their land and found hope in America.

They consecrated America by making a *covenant* with the LORD that He is the God of our nation and that we are His people. This covenant was made manifest by the first act of Jamestown Settlers (the first permanent English settlement) in 1607, when they prayed and firmly planted a tall, wooden cross at their Virginia landing site, declaring to all generations that Jesus Christ and America were joined in covenant.[1]

The Pilgrims likewise covenanted our nation to God for His glory and the advancement of the Christian faith. The Puritans, John Hancock, George Washington, and others continued to consecrate our nation to God through prayer, our Declaration of Independence, and the Constitution.

Our founders understood that a united America living as "one nation under God" was His blueprint and desire. This was more than doing their own plans and asking God to bless them; they daily sought God's will. As Christians of many denominations, they prayed and worked together to unify the USA in Christ—"united we stand!"

Abraham Lincoln along with our founders believed that our nation would be blessed as long as we maintained our relationship with Jesus. As president, Lincoln proclaimed, *Recognize the sublime truth, announced in the Holy Scriptures and proven by all history, that those nations only are blessed whose God is the Lord.*[2]

As a nation, we have seen more of Heaven on earth than those living in any other country. Serving God has given us His uncommon freedom and made the USA the leader among nations, with His extraordinary provision, wisdom, and protection.

> **HOLY BIBLE** **Bible Principle**
>
> *Americans have experienced more of Heaven on earth than other nations.*

The true American dream is stated with the New England Confederation in 1643. It reminds us that *we all came into these parts of America with one and the same end and aim, namely, to advance the Kingdom of our Lord Jesus Christ and to enjoy the liberties of the Gospel in purity with peace.*[3] Nothing is more American than Christian religious liberty!

Blessings Come By Following God's Plan

John Hancock is one of the most respected men in our free country who risked his life for our Christian liberty. One could say he is the first modern American as he signed the Declaration of Independence first with the largest signature as president of the fearless Continental Congress. Like our other forefathers, he believed government serves Jesus Christ.

As governor of Massachusetts, he led the people in exalting our Lord in 1791 by saying, *The great and most important Blessing, the Gospel of Jesus Christ... that all may bow to the scepter of our LORD JESUS CHRIST...*[4] Leaders serving God give Americans confidence of doing God's will.

Some may be surprised to discover how strongly John Hancock, George Washington, John Adams, and our founders sought God and relied on Him for our nation. Many don't know these truths about combining God and country because of a long-term and subtle strategy by the father of lies to remove Christianity from our nation's children.

Putting God First Makes A Happier Life

Following Jesus is what brings abundant life, individually and nationally. This is the only way to come out of darkness, for Jesus is the Light of the world (John 8:12).

Our history shows that there are higher employment rates, better jobs, and the dollar has a greater value when our nation seeks first the Kingdom of God and His righteousness.[5,6] Americans had no income tax until 1913 because bold Christians and pastors called for righteousness. Imagine keeping your whole paycheck (Matthew 6:33)!

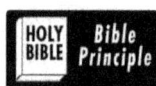

HOLY BIBLE *Bible Principle*

The USA serving Jesus Christ results in greater wealth and less taxes.

We have happier lives when the USA puts our Lord first. More people stay married when with the Bible in society. Part of the reason comes from Christian encouragement to find God's answers to marriage issues, including forgiveness and faithfulness. Earlier generations found Biblical ways to work out family challenges and keep their marriage covenants.

Jesus gives us purpose in life, and living for Him helps children find God's plan. Children are better educated and have fewer troubles when taught the Bible because the Holy

Spirit fills their lives with wisdom, understanding, and knowledge (Proverbs 1). Also our family and friends are more likely to go to Heaven by trusting in Jesus Christ for their salvation when the government promotes the Gospel. Christians are honored and not persecuted. The whole nation is safer since God protects us from evil by trusting in Him.

The best national security program is one that establishes a structure where we abide with God in our personal lives and as a nation as Psalm 91 assures. Here the psalmist confidently trusts in God's impenetrable protection from evil. He was pursued and persecuted, yet he found that no army, terrorist, or calamity can come against those who trust in God. The preeminent strategy of wicked leaders is to destroy trust in God. Tyranny is easy, if God is removed from the hearts and minds of the people. But faith in God always defeats tyrants.

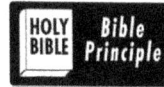

HOLY BIBLE *Bible Principle*

Serving the LORD only frees the USA of oppression and Shariah law.

The blessings of Heaven determine the difference between peace and war. The Kingdom of God frees us from dictators, Shariah law, a secular world government, communism, and other non-Christian ways.

The Holy Spirit fills our country when the people of this great nation choose to draw near to God. As we abide in Christ and His Words abide in us, we dwell with God (John 15:7). God's presence is seen in having the freedom and security we desire. Christian love, wisdom, forgiveness, and truth are from God.

It is right to believe that Christianity is God's only agenda for the USA. Our founders wanted every American to read the Bible. So Congress affirmed they *highly approve the pious and laudable undertaking... as subservient to the interest of [Christian] religion... in this country, and... they recommend this edition of the bible to the inhabitants of the United*

States.[7] Our second president, John Adams reminds us, *The Christian religion is, above all the religions...[8]* The freedom to practice Christianity assures the best way to make disciples.

Additional reasons for Americans to do God's will and to rally together and defend Christianity as a nation are:

- Following Jesus Christ is what makes the USA one of God's greatest assets on earth
- Eliminating terrorism
- Freedom from a police state (i.e. the militarization of the police force, restricting free speech, martial law...)
- Ridding our country of IRS corruption, and school violence
- Removing the dangers from the enormous debt

Is God Judging the USA?

God is doing all He can to tell us to turn to Him. We will discover this by looking at His Word to find the truth of what is happening in our country, why things don't feel right, and how He says to fix things. Just as parents discipline disobedient children, God disciplines those who disobey His Word. God is the Judge of all, both individuals and nations. The USA is blessed for obeying God and suffers when we sin.

God says, *When the land sins against Me... then will I stretch out Mine hand upon it, and... will send famine upon it* (Ezekiel 14:13). His judgments on a nation take many forms. While we look at His discipline, we should hold on to hope because this book explains how to end God's judgment!

As we learn God's blueprint to save our nation, we will look at three hidden, yet remarkable, Bible accounts that give God's answer for America's future. They are King Asa, King Josiah, and Moses (2 Chronicles 15 & 34, Exodus 32).

With so many wars, terrorists, riots, and division, there seems to be a similarity for us to King Asa's day when "there was no peace... nation was destroyed of nation, and city of city" (2 Chronicles 15:5-6). But Asa found hope that God was with Judah while they were with Him; and if they sought

Him, He would be found. God would free them of the trouble. He also knew that God was righteous and if they forsook God, He would forsake them (2 Chronicles 15:2). King Josiah followed in King Asa's footsteps of renewing covenant and loving God and the greatest revival came with King Josiah. The entire nation turned to God.

When God was ready to destroy Israel for worshipping the golden calf, Moses reminded God of His great mercy and covenant with Israel. Moses separated the people by finding out who loved God and who didn't by asking: *Who is on the LORD'S side?* (Exodus 32:10-26)

Likewise, true American leaders lead us to follow God. Encouraging our country to be on God's side, John Adams said, *As the safety and prosperity of nations ultimately and essentially depend on the protection and the blessing of Almighty God... the just judgments of God against prevalent iniquity, are a loud call to repentance and reformation...*[9]

Famous John Winthrop, who applied "a city on a hill" to America, said, *If we... shall embrace this present world... then the Lord will surely break out in wrath against us... He will make us know the price of the breach of such a covenant.*[10]

To win the revolutionary war for our freedom, George Washington knew the USA must avoid provoking God, so he said, *We cannot hope for the blessing of heaven on our army if we insult it by our impiety and folly.*[11] It is encouraging that God has a way for us to be blessed!

The Real Reason for Our Crisis

Some say judgment is coming or it is reserved for a future catastrophic end of the world, but the Bible shows that the USA is already under severe judgment for our great sins. This is the real reason why so many in our nation are concerned for our future, Christians have been persecuted, and we are in danger. The judgments are worse than most imagined and few know what God says will end our judgment.

Others believe that God's chastisement is an Old Testament idea. They say we live in New Testament times where its about forgiveness and grace, but is that Biblical? While Jesus' sacrifice does provide forgiveness and God's grace, it does not eliminate God's discipline if we oppose Him.

The New Testament says judgment begins at the house of God (1 Peter 4:17). Jesus Christ teaches that judgment comes to those not repenting of sin (Revelation 2:20-23). We see how Ananias, Sapphira, and Herod died from disobeying God (Acts 5:1-10; 12:23). Abraham Lincoln reminds us, *by His divine law, nations like individuals are subjected to punishments and chastisements...*[12]

The good news is God always has a way out of every problem. He asks this generation of our nation to give Him all of our hearts so He will bless us (Galatians 6:7-8).

Jesus Christ said our first responsibility is to *love the LORD your God...* (Mark 12:30). For this reason, those who made our country raised American children to love and follow God. Public schools educated children with, *The love of God comprehends the love of all his attributes—the love of his justice in condemning and punishing sin—as well as of his mercy in forgiving and saving penitent sinners...* [13]

In presidential proclamations, George Washington taught, *It is the duty of nations... to obey His will,*[14] and Abraham Lincoln shared, *It is the duty of nations as well as of men, to own their dependence upon the overruling power of God.*[15]

The most satisfying life is from doing God's will. Have you made the wise decision to follow Jesus Christ and not a false god? Do you want the USA to follow Jesus? By deciding that the LORD is our God, you have the assurance of His special favor, both personally and for our nation.

Our founders were willing to sacrifice everything so they and their children could live securely in a nation where they could freely follow Jesus Christ. Prayer was given at the foundation of this great country and it is our duty to continue this holy mission and to have God as our first priority. We will learn what the Bible says has caused our crisis and what the roadmap is to restore God's extraordinary blessings to us.

20

✝ *Prayer*

Father, I follow You, and I want the USA
to follow You and to have Your blessings,
not Your judgment. In Jesus' name. Amen.

✓ *Summary and Reflection Questions*

The 7 Bible Truths in this book are the exact same principles that make you a strong Christian and bring God's favor to you, when you personalize the Bible Truths to your life. No matter what challenges you may face, these timeless truths will also help you be blessed with every good gift that God desires to give you.

As a nation, God rewarded our founders by making the USA the greatest nation because they joined God and country together. Our nation serving God means we have lives that are extraordinarily blessed. However, He has been judging our nation for disobeying Him. Following God's plan for the USA is how we live a happier life with Christian liberty, all our needs met, protection, and peace!

1. *How has God blessed the USA? Why?*
2. *In what ways do you have a better life when the USA follows Jesus Christ?*
3. *What are Biblical examples of God judging nations?*
4. *Do you want our country to serve the LORD? Why?*

2

Signs and Wonders of Judgment

*"Go, inquire of the LORD... for great is the
wrath of the LORD that is poured out upon us..."*
2 Chronicles 34:21

What would cause King Josiah to rip his clothes upon hearing God's Word? Josiah lived in a world where the Word of God was set aside and forgotten. He loved God and wanted to honor Him so he commissioned the repairing of God's temple.

Suddenly the Law of God was found in the recesses of the temple and the priests brought it to the king. For the first time in his life Josiah heard these words and saw the connection between the nation's sins and God's judgment. What he heard opened his eyes. He trembled as he realized that he was not truly honoring God by allowing evil to remain and God was going to bring total destruction for their sin. Seeing that God's judgment was on Judah, he tore his clothes in desperation and fear. He ordered the false gods to be destroyed and led the people to serve the LORD and turn from evil.

When Josiah inquired of God, he discovered the reasons for their problems and learned that their lives were at risk for forsaking God (2 Chronicles 34:21). King Josiah said, "For great is the wrath of the LORD that is kindled against us for our fathers did not follow God's Word" (2 Kings 22:13).

Will we have the same tender heart of love for God, humble ourselves, and repent? Amazingly, the nation's greatest revival came with Josiah after the evil King Manasseh and many others forgot God.

To understand the magnitude of the danger before us for breaking God's laws as a nation, let's look at what God says about this. We know that God is holy and He judges sin. Starting with the fall of man, the Bible reveals that sin brings curses. Certain sins bring specific judgments and Biblical curses *for a sign and for a wonder* that we would know that God is judging us (Deuteronomy 28:46). These outcomes are designed so we have godly sorrow and repent.

As we look at current events, we see many news stories are Biblical signs and wonders revealing that the USA is under God's judgment for our sins and is in danger of destruction unless our nation immediately turns to God. His judgments are *true and righteous* (Revelation 16:7). Like our founders, we are to have a holy fear of God, since sin affects our lives, finances, and environment (Romans 1:18).

Judgment: Spoiling, Debt, and More Taxes

Caused by those who: (1) Disobey God's Word; (2) Reject our founders' covenant / don't want the Bible in schools; (3) Turn to unbelievers for leaders / have strange gods; (4) Abort children; and (5) Use the occult. 2 Kings 17:15-20.

Spoiling, or plundering, is when government, businesses, foreigners, or people take our wealth by high taxes, debts, housing crashes, and other losses (Deut. 28:29). The 2017 debt estimate is $20.241 trillion according to the Government Printing Office (GPO).[1] This is approximately double the $10 trillion owed in 2009. The enormous loss of money owed to the Federal Reserve and other countries should get our attention. The debt is a serious danger to our national security. If the dollar collapses, there would be a financial crisis and large riots could cause deaths, such as what Greece experienced with austerity taxes and devaluing its money.[2]

God says if a nation disobeys His Word, the judgment is foreigners *shall lend to you, and you shall not lend to him: he shall be the head, and you shall be the tail* (Deut. 28:44).

Our blessed Christian nation was founded with no personal, sales, or other taxes that are common today. Taxes like inheritance tax, federal income tax, FICA, and Obamacare taxes would be seen as unjust by our founders since they are plundering. High corporate taxes are causing businesses to move to foreign countries with lower taxes.[3]

The USA has gone from having more than half the wealth of the world to now having nearly 80% of the people live near poverty, with joblessness or a reliance on welfare for at least part of their lives.[4] The USA lowered to second place in the world economy for the first time since 1872, as based on purchasing power parity (PPP), while first based on GDP?[5]

The loss of so much money is not just greedy politicians, but it is caused from every individual person not repenting.

> *[They] rejected His statutes [God's Word], and His covenant that He made with their fathers... they... went after the heathen... and worshipped all the host of heaven... they caused their sons and their daughters to pass through the fire [to kill as in abortion], and used divination... Therefore the LORD... delivered them into the hand of spoilers* (2 Kings 17:15-20 KJV).

God wants us to stop losing our savings and retirement income as a country. Taxes are so high because of disobeying God. The reason that conservative politicians can't remove the national debt is because it is a judgment from God caused by our sins. To end a judgment requires confessing and repenting of the sin that caused it and having Jesus' blood cover us (Genesis 3:16-19, Revelation 22:3, 1 John 1:7, Proverbs 26:2).

In many ways God has sold the USA to our enemies for having other gods. *The anger of the LORD was hot against Israel, and He delivered them into the hands of spoilers that spoiled them, and He sold them into the hands of their enemies* (Judges 2:14). But we have hope, for God delivered Israel when they turned to Him (Judges 2:16-18).

Judgment:
They That Hate You Shall Reign Over You

Caused by those who: (1) Oppose the USA following the Holy Bible, and (2) Commit covenant breaking acts, i.e. to vote for non-Christians, abortion, etc. Leviticus 26:17. Psalm 106:35-42

Most people disapprove of politicians.[6] Millions have protested corruption, unjust wars, and using our money to support foreigners with little success. Why do politicians betray us? God says, *If your soul abhors My judgments* and you *break My covenant: I also will do this unto you... they that hate you shall reign over you* (Leviticus 26:14-17).

He further warns, *I will... deliver you into the hand of brutish men, and skillful to destroy* (Ezekiel 21:31). We see this with the mess in Washington where politicians have not listened to the people. Those opposing our Christian founders, such as Muslims, Al-Qaeda, atheists, gays, and abortionists, scheme against us, as Barack Obama helps them.[7] Obama disregards the Constitution and omits references to God in the Declaration of Independence and our National Motto.[8] These are acts of hatred to Americans. Even before Obama, politicians against the USA have been God's judgment.

Violating the Constitution with same-sex marriage shows the five Supreme Court justices' and Obama's hatred to Americans with a premeditated attack on Christians. We know that God will destroy the USA if people don't oppose this sin. God, the Supreme Judge, promises that the land "vomits out" those given to homosexual and other sins. He removes sodomite societies from the earth (Acts 5:29, Lev.

18:25). It is one thing for a gay person to disobey God and be judged individually, but if a nation supports gay sin, the nation is destroyed (2 Peter 2:6, Romans 1:24-32, Ezekiel 23).

The news exposed how the Obamacare architect exploited words to hide more taxes and insulted voters as "stupid" who supported it.[9] Obama lied that costs would be less for healthcare and that people could keep their doctors and plans.[10] Millions of people pay costly Obamacare fines and have been cut from full-time to part-time work. Death panels that dishonor the elderly and others by choosing who not to treat were once denied but are now admitted.[11] Obamacare gives businesses a $3,000 incentive to hire illegal aliens instead of Americans[12] and Christian hospitals are closing.

Since God uses brutal people in judgment, that explains why we see China, Muslims, North Korea, Iran, and others lining up against us. God says, *I will bring the worst of the heathen* in judgment (Ezekiel 7:24 KJV) and *The LORD shall bring a nation against you from afar, from the end of the earth... a nation whose language you shall not understand, a nation of fierce countenance, which shall not regard the old, nor show favor to the young* (Deuteronomy 28:49-50).

The bright spot is when Israel *cried unto the LORD, the LORD raised up a deliverer...who delivered them* (Judges 3:9). God gives excellent leaders when the people do His will, but fierce oppressors for disobedience (Judges 2-5). It is urgent to humble ourselves and cry out to God for deliverance.

"Those who hate you shall reign over you" is often seen in the Bible. To study further, see Psalm 106:35-42, Isaiah 19:4 & 42:24, Ezekiel 23:28-30, Leviticus 26:40-41, and Judges 2-4.

Judgment: Foreigners Rising Above Americans

Caused by those who: (1) Disobey God's Word, (2) Shed blood, (3) Lie and Rob, (4) Have false gods, (5) Practice witchcraft. Deut. 28:43; Nahum 3:1-13.

Foreigners taking away jobs (about 50% of all new jobs added went to foreign born workers since 2009[13]) and banning the American flag are costly judgments for not keeping the Word of God. They canceled America Day at Jackson Hole High School in Wyoming to not offend foreign groups.[14]

Concerns abound with over 195,900 illegal alien criminals released to the USA.[15] There are over 100,000 deaths from illegal aliens, said a father whose son was killed by one not deported.[16] A woman was killed by an illegal alien with seven felonies that the San Francisco Sheriff wouldn't deport.[17]

But it shall come to pass, if you will not hear the voice of the LORD your God... that all these curses shall come upon you, and overtake you... The fruit of your land, and all your labors, shall a nation which you know not eat up; and you shall be only oppressed and crushed always... The foreigner that is within you shall get up above you very high; and you shall come down very low (Deuteronomy 28:15, 33, 43).

How can we be safe with a dangerous open border allowing in enemies, gangs, disease, terrorists, and those not identifying with our Christian nation? We can't have a country without borders. Being unprotected and Muslims who scheme to illegally overthrow our Constitution with Shariah law are a sign for us that our nation is at risk (Leviticus 26:38).

The bloody city... full of lies and robbery... because of the multitude of the whoredoms... witchcrafts... the gates of your land shall be set wide open unto your enemies (Nahum 3:1-13).

Judgment: Terrorism

Caused by those who: (1) Disobey God's Word, and (2) Break covenant with strange gods, vote for worldly people, state the USA is not a Christian nation, forbid Christian prayer in schools, etc. Leviticus 26:14-16.

God does promise to protect His people, yet terrorism hasn't ended because the Bible teaches that terror is a curse from our sin. Trillions of dollars will never stop terrorism as it is God's judgment. *If... ye will not do all My commandments, but that ye break My covenant: I also will do this unto you; I will even appoint over you terror* (Leviticus 26:14-16).

Instead of targeting terrorists against our nation, the "Department of Homeland Security" (DHS) called Christians, pro-lifers, veterans, and patriotic Americans possible

27

terrorists.[18] The DHS Secretary mocked our founding fathers by stating the Islamic Koran has "quintessential American values,"[19] but our Christian founders followed the Holy Bible. Disobeying God's Word and tolerance of other gods is the main cause for 9/11 and the unpopular Patriot Act that has been used for unconstitutional spying. Many fear the full terror judgment of being slain by enemies and fleeing when no one pursues, so it is urgent we call on God as these judgments are sounding off like sirens (Leviticus 26:17).

Our nation is a Christian nation and many do not realize that it provokes God if people state the USA is not a Christian nation. Disloyalty and unbelief result in God's continued judgment on the USA as He views it as a break in covenant.

Judgment: Lost Freedom

Caused by those who: (1) Disobey God's Word and (2) Don't forsake their wicked works (i.e. voting for the ungodly, strange gods, idols, abortion, etc.). Nehemiah 9:34-37, Ezekiel 16:36-37.

Many are concerned by tyranny increasing, a police state, and communist threats. While we want liberty, losing freedom at first and then being servants is another of God's judgments.

Neither have our kings, our princes, our priests, nor our fathers, kept your law... neither turned they from their wicked works. Behold, we are servants this day, and for the land that you gave unto our fathers... we are servants in it: And it yields much increase unto the kings whom you have set over us because of our sins: also they have dominion over our bodies, and over our cattle, at their pleasure, and we are in great distress (Nehemiah 9:34-37).

Public shame of our nation is a judgment. The USA's nakedness is being displayed as people watch filthy movies, teenagers share indecent photos of themselves on their phones, and at airports there are "naked body scanners" and the patting down and groping of innocent Americans. While some of this exposure is from people's own choice, part of it is judgment.

He says, *Through your whoredoms with your lovers, and with all the idols of your abominations, and by the blood of your children, which you did give unto them... therefore I will gather all your lovers... and will uncover your nakedness unto them, that they may see all your nakedness* (Ezekiel 16:36-37). And, *I will uncover your skirts upon your face, and I will show the nations your nakedness* (Nahum 3:5).

We have only seen the first signs and wonders of this judgment, so we must consider the danger before us, get on our knees, and ask God for mercy. The full judgment is to be taken captive and killed (Ezekiel 16:38-41).

Our privacy is being compromised as a judgment. For example, the National Security Administration (NSA) and others secretly activate our own cameras and microphones on cell phones and Internet-connected TV's and devices. They record our lives in our own bedrooms and living rooms.

Personal phone calls, emails, web surfing, chat sessions, and social media are scanned and/or read without probable cause or warrants.[20] Cars are tracked[21] and privacy is taken away by police state monitoring. Random traffic stops are illegal Fourth Amendment violations (unwarranted searches) where the innocent are treated without dignity or like criminals. God says our national security comes from trusting in Him not by giving up our liberty (Psalm 33:16-18, 146:3-5).

Judgment: Economic Decline, Famine, and Earth and Animals Harmed

Caused by those not turning from their wicked ways (no truth, nor mercy, nor knowledge of God, swearing, lying, killing, stealing, adultery, homosexuality, etc.). 2 Chronicles 7:13-14, Hosea 4:1-3, Genesis 19:24-25

The next judgments are drought, bad crops, pestilence, and failed businesses (Deuteronomy 28:15 & 40, 2 Samuel 21:1). God says, *If I shut up heaven that there be no rain, or if I command the locusts to devour... or if I send pestilence... If My people, which are called by My name, shall humble themselves, and pray, and seek My face, and turn from their wicked ways; then will I hear from heaven, and will forgive their sin, and will heal their land* (2 Chronicles 7:13-14 KJV).

The only way to protect creation is for our country to turn from our sins. Great devastation to the environment came by God's judgment on sin with Noah's flood, the plagues in Egypt, and the cities of the plain being destroyed.

The Bible teaches that ruin to the environment is caused by wickedness, rebellion to God, thinking on evil, and homosexual sin (Genesis 6:5-17; 19:24-28, Exodus 7:14-11:10). Throughout Scripture sin is what causes judgment on the earth and animals. *Because there is no truth, nor mercy, nor knowledge of God in the land. By swearing, and lying, and killing, and stealing, and committing adultery... Therefore shall the land mourn, and every one that dwells therein shall languish, with the beasts of the field, and with the fowls of heaven; yes, the fishes of the sea also shall be taken away.* (Hosea 4:1-3). But the Holy Spirit gives life to creation when we follow God.

Instead of focusing on the environment and being "green," our priority is to live a holy life. We are to fear God, for He controls the climate, not man; He has promised to not destroy the earth, but He will judge the people sinning (Genesis 8:22).

Judgment:
The Ungodly Turning on Christians
Caused by those who turn to ungodly people in politics, business, and religious circles. Ezekiel 23:5 & 9.

Unbelievers persecuting Christians is from God's people turning to them. We see this judgment by Christians losing jobs at companies that defy God with diversity for gays, the mayors who tried to ban Chick-fil-A for believing in traditional marriage, and from non-Christian school boards picking sinful curriculum with evolution and abortion, which harms children's souls. We also see this with Obama and other ungodly people wanting men to enter women's bathrooms, which endangers young children, women, and everyone.[22]

She was Mine; and she lusted on her lovers... Therefore I have delivered her into the hand of her lovers, into the hand of the Assyrians, upon whom she lusted (Ezekiel 23:5, 9).

30

Jesus Christ says, *by their fruit you shall know them* (Matthew 7:16). This is why Jesus tells us Obama is not a Christian. Obama's fruit is persecuting Christians, hiding crosses in the military and at Georgetown, removing Bible verses, and promoting false gods, abortion, and same-sex sin.[23]

We know God blesses the USA because of the Christians, not the ungodly, as the Bible teaches. For Christians to be honored, we must only support those truly serving Jesus.

The People Not Repenting Cause Our Judgment

God wants to help us. That is why He tells us that those not following Jesus Christ and the Bible are the ones causing our troubles, from corruption to terrorism. It is one thing to unintentionally sin and then confess the sin and be forgiven, but to publicly support sin or to not repent provokes God.

We all benefit from understanding why God judges. The judgments are caused by those people who won't repent of:

- False gods
- Not calling for Christian religious liberty
- Not standing up for our God-given rights of life, liberty, the pursuit of happiness, property, and conscience
- Removing God from government, schools, courts, and the military
- Helping non-Christians in politics and business
- Abortion
- Unjust wars
- Coveting (wanting other people's items, greed)
- Homosexuality, adultery, and fornication
- The occult, sorcery, and witchcraft

These are nation destroying sins; God sees them as covenant breaking acts. That is why we must repent, for sin is the greatest enemy we have. The strength of our military and all our wealth cannot defend against God's anger for these sins. He can easily defeat our strongest defense. Our consciences should remind us that sin is treason against God.

31

We cannot be deceived if TV and news shows downplay these sins as only social issues or a culture war. For example, the news says the focus is the economy, but God says obeying Him is the focus, because sin is what causes an economic collapse. This is why the true battle to save the USA is between those following Jesus Christ and those not following Him. The right opposing the left and the left opposing the right is not God's plan, for both tolerate some of these sins. The USA's highest priority is to end God's judgment.

The Decision: Who Will Follow God?

Storm clouds have wreaked havoc on our nation as they have crept through the land destroying what was in their path. The devil is also against our nation that is consecrated to God. Jesus said the thief comes "to steal, and to kill, and to destroy: I am come that they might have life" (John 10:10). By the USA exalting Jesus and honoring Christians, the devil flees from our nation and we have Christian liberty (James 4:7).

Our hope is to turn to God right now, for in Noah's day final judgment came quickly when most didn't expect it. We know when Sodom and Gomorrah went "after strange flesh," unashamed of gay sin, then "the LORD rained upon Sodom and upon Gomorrah brimstone and fire from the LORD out of heaven" (Genesis 19:24). Our hearts are to be tender to God like Josiah who rent his clothes in fear and shame when he found out the nation wasn't following God's Word.

The only real solution for survival is national repentance. Without repentance God says, *I also walk contrary unto you, and will punish you yet seven times for your sins* (Leviticus 26:24). Punishing seven times more occurs four times in Leviticus 26 when people rebel against God. That is why we must repent right away. A final judgment could include being taken captive as slaves (Deuteronomy 28:68).

Hope: God's Answer Is the 7 Bible Truths

The good news is those who think it's over for America have forgotten God's mercy. Nineveh had just forty days until destruction in Jonah's day, but the people humbled themselves

32

before God and He spared them. While God is just and judges, we have the hope of His forgiveness for He is also merciful and slow to anger. He doesn't want to destroy our country for our sins. God wants to show mercy to the USA! His loving purpose in giving us time to repent is for us to have a change of heart and decide to follow Him. After all, no one would respect a judge who let the unrepentant go free.

Some people pray for God to judge our country more so that our nation repents, but we know God doesn't desire more punishment just as earthly parents do not relish punishing their children. God says, *Woe unto you that desire the day of the LORD! to what end is it for you? the day of the LORD is darkness, and not light* (Amos 5:18 KJV).

To save the USA, instead of praying for judgment, we are to pray for the Holy Spirit to fill the USA so we have a deep sense of conviction of our sins. We are to cry out for godly sorrow to fill our nation so we repent of indifference about immorality on TV, trying to fix the economy without following God, shedding innocent blood, and other sins. Praying for our nation's hearts to love God more brings revival (John 15:14).

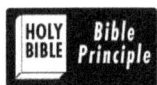

HOLY BIBLE *Bible Principle*

Pray for the Holy Spirit to fill the USA.

Not everyone repents with more judgment (Rev. 16:9-11). If the troubles of the 9/11 catastrophe, the economic downturn, losing liberties, and other judgments haven't caused people to fear God and to depart from evil, then it is possible that more judgments would not bring true repentance. Many have listened to lying spirits and must awake out of deception (2 Chronicles 18:21).

We have already seen many of the judgments for trusting in heathen leaders instead of God for help, such as being delivered into the unbeliever's hands (Ezekiel 23:9). The next judgments are extreme, for God says the final judgments are to lose our children and to be invaded with total destruction or the removal of the USA (Ezekiel 22:30). *They took her sons and her daughters, and slew her with the sword... for they had executed judgment upon her* (Ezekiel 23:10 KJV).

We are to thank God that He is merciful. Turning to Him will stop His judgment. When He sees hearts that obediently love Him, He will: (1) Go back, which is to hold back; (2) Spare, or (3) Repent from judgment, as He did with kings Asa and Josiah when Judah turned to Him (Ezekiel 24:14). Amos asked God to repent from the judgments that He said He would do and God listened to Amos' requests (Amos 7:1-6).

I ask God for mercy for the USA continually. I stand in agreement that our nation is forgiven by the shed blood of Jesus Christ as I have dedicated myself to pastoring our nation with teaching and repentance to end judgment. Could it be that Israel was taken captive when Jeremiah stopped asking God for mercy? (Jeremiah 18:21-23) We are tempted to have a heart like Jonah opposing mercy for Nineveh, but we need a shepherd's heart like Jesus and Moses.

HOLY BIBLE *Bible Principle*

God's answer for America's future is found on another tree at Calvary.

Reading this book provides the step-by-step plan of how God will heal our land. The *7 Bible Truths* that you are now going to discover teach you what removes all these judgments. Each truth makes your life and America stronger.

God's *7 Bible Truths* will: restore our wealth, lower taxes, and remove the debt; give leaders who love Americans; make the USA great again; secure our borders; end terrorism; give liberty, privacy, and all our God-given rights; and protect the earth and animals. They restore families and are instrumental to bring the Third Great Awakening, where multitudes are convicted of how great our sins have been before a holy God.

These *Bible Truths* are God's answer for the books *The Harbinger,* a warning sign, and *Shemitah*, a Hebrew word for the seven year cycle of rest and release. *The Harbinger* is from the Isaiah 9:10 analogy of the bricks falling and the sycamore tree being cut down. But God's answer for America's future is found on another tree—the more significant tree at Calvary. Four verses before we find God's answer, *the government shall be upon His [Jesus'] shoulder* (Isaiah 9:6); the cross at Calvary gives us mercy and grace.

I believe the greatest miraculous comeback for America is happening now as more people discover what they can do in God's plan. I believe that America is not going to fall. We already see some signs of hope. The USA is going to be saved because of those who are on God's side. By agreeing with the *7 Bible Truths* found in the rest of this book, you show God that the USA is on His side.

What you will now learn is guaranteed to change your future and restore great blessings. Teaching these urgently needed truths from God is how you and your church can help.

✝ *Prayer*

Father, You are merciful. Americans humble ourselves and confess our sins. We cry out to You to end Your judgments by Your great mercy. In Jesus' name. Amen.

✓ *Summary and Reflection Questions*

We find hope in God giving us signs and wonders of His judgment so we repent and avoid more trouble. His discipline shows that we are still His people (Hebrews 12:5-7).

Everyone who turns to God heals our land. But our nation's real problem is those people who are unwilling to follow God, as the Bible teaches sinners cause His judgment. Be encouraged—God wants to show mercy to the USA.

1. *What sins caused God's judgment to our country?*
2. *Read Leviticus 26:15 and 17. Explain what "they that hate you shall reign over you" means.*
3. *If you want to have God's blessings, will you confess and turn from your sins?*
4. *God is merciful and just. Why does He judge nations?*

35

3

First Truth—America's 7 Secrets:
Choose the True God...

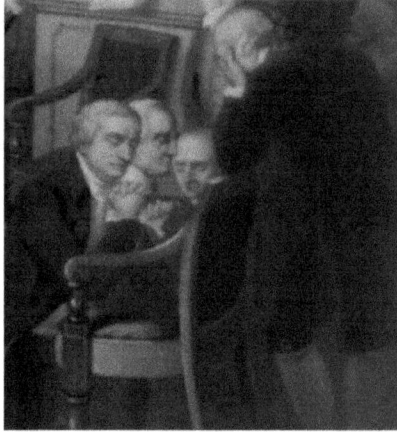

The founding fathers serving the LORD in Congress.
John Jay, first Chief Justice, is second from left.

"The secret of the LORD is with those who fear Him;
and He will show them His covenant." Psalm 25:14

Americans have stood far above all other nations with freedom and prosperity. But how did the USA gain this favor from God? What did our founders do? If we do what they did, would God bless us the same today?

The understanding of God's ongoing blessings for America was once common knowledge since Jesus is the Author of Liberty. America's secrets have since been hidden from many but they are certainly not lost.

In order to find out why God blesses America, we need to ask, who made the USA? The answer is Christians—but not ordinary Christians. The founders were mature Christians seeking to glorify God in the country they were building.

There are seven American secrets needed to make the USA great again. These secrets are the core beliefs that the famed pastors who founded America established our nation on. Much of our country's crisis and dangers are because these principles are missing from our churches and daily lives.

Following these beliefs will also make our churches exceptional; great churches are what make the USA great. Therefore, every Christian must quickly share these beliefs.

The 7 Beliefs of True American Pastors ✝🇺🇸

Christian Religious Liberty
The USA serves the LORD.
Matthew 4:10 & 12:30, Galatians 5:1

One Nation Under God
The USA is a covenant Christian nation.
Psalm 33:12, Jamestown Settlers, Pilgrims...

God-given Rights
Life, liberty, the pursuit of happiness,
conscience and property. Genesis 1:27, Lev. 25:10

The Gospel of Jesus Christ
Christ died for our sins, was buried, rose again...
1 Corinthians 15:3-8, Mark 12:30-31

Righteousness Exalts the USA
No false gods, be pro-life, traditional marriage only... Proverbs 14:34

Jesus Christ Leads the Government
It is the duty of nations to obey God.
Isaiah 9:6 & 33:22

Christian Disciple Making As a Nation
The Bible in schools, chaplains pray in Jesus' name... as Jesus and our founders teach.
Matthew 28:19-20

The respected founding pastors taught these beliefs to our founders to advance the Kingdom of God. The 7 Bible Truths, which include these 7 beliefs, are what make America exceptional.

Secret 1: Call for Christian Religious Liberty

Our founders understood God's First Commandment is to love the LORD so they made freedom to serve Jesus Christ the USA's number one priority. The USA and Israel have in common that both demanded to serve the LORD as a country, even when tyrants, such as King George and Pharaoh, said no.

God abundantly blessed our founders for demanding their Christian liberty to freely worship Him by freeing the USA from England. This is like how God freed Israel from slavery. If you want oppression removed, then have faith, for God is against tyranny. He fought for His people, undoing the Egyptian's chariot wheels in the Red Sea (Exodus 14:25). Since God is against tyranny, Christians also oppose it.

The USA and Israel both have the greatest political leaders in history. God defines a leader as a just man "ruling in the fear of God" (2 Samuel 23:3). Among Israel's leaders are Moses and kings Asa and Josiah who brought revival. Our founders mentioned in this book are many of America's premiere leaders, along with the pastors who taught them.

A well known preacher, Declaration signer, and a ratifier of the Constitution, John Witherspoon, said, *Whoever is an avowed enemy of God, I scruple not to call him an enemy to his country.*[1] The colonial clergy *were men not only of eminent piety... but were ardent lovers of liberty,*[2] shared historian Benjamin Morris. Deep in our hearts and churches is pure love for God. America's first secret is pastors insisting the USA has Christian religious liberty to serve the LORD.

We must only stand up for *Christian religious liberty* to serve the LORD, not religious liberty of false gods. The reason is so we don't provoke God (2 Chronicles 34:25). Our Christian founders typically used the word "religion" to mean Christianity, since the King James Version of the Bible does this (James 1:26-27). When we read our founding fathers saying "religious liberty," they typically mean "Christian liberty". They put the Holy Bible in public schools to prove this.

> **HOLY BIBLE** *Bible Principle*
>
> *Never let anyone take away your God-given rights.*

It is dangerous to serve other gods. If Moses had said, "Israel must have liberty for Baal and also the LORD," then God would have killed Moses for forsaking Him. God calls the USA to worship Him only, not strange gods (Exodus 32).

Secret 2:
The USA Is a Covenant Christian Nation

Our founding fathers made the LORD the USA's God, which is the foundation of our country. Their desire to freely follow God is why He delivered them from government persecution of Christians in Europe, just as the history of the Israelites demonstrates the many times that God freed them from persecution from other government states.

America's journey to freedom is much like Israel's deliverance out of bondage in Egypt and their journey into the promised land. Our founders also found a promised land "to enjoy the liberties of the gospel".[3] What do the USA and Israel have in common? Both are covenant nations to the LORD from the start. Our God is a covenant God.

No other nation has the same covenant with Jesus Christ that the USA has with God. We are unique and our founders' covenant to follow the LORD is the second American secret.

Israel's covenant is through Abraham and continued with Moses. Other nations became Christian nations, but America made a covenant to God through Jesus Christ from the start.

First Bible Truth to end God's judgment Psalm 33:12, 2 Cor. 6:16	Re-affirm Covenant: The LORD is the God of the USA and Americans are His people
	Why? To get our nation in right relationship with God.

Bible Blessings: How to Guarantee God Will Save the USA and Bless You

The First Bible Truth is to re-affirm our covenant that the USA serves the LORD. This guarantees God will save our nation and bless you, making Americans (those in covenant) God's special people. Choosing the LORD as our God gets us in right relationship with Him.

The current generation in the USA must be brought into covenant. To receive the blessings of covenant we must belong to God. We give God everything and He gives us everything. He doesn't give His favored blessings to those not in covenant (1 Peter 2:9, Deuteronomy 26:18).

If you join our founders' covenant with God, you have God's blessings for our nation through what they did in Christ; otherwise, you have to start over. While I was growing up almost everyone said, "I am a Christian because I am an American." Christianity is our identity. The LORD being our God is the light at the end of the tunnel—the first step to end judgment.

When Kings Asa and Josiah made covenant, God's favor returned to Judah. *They entered into a covenant to seek the LORD God of their fathers with all their heart and with all their soul* (2 Chronicles 15:12).

God wants a covenant for it defines who are His people. A covenant is holy and unbreakable. Having great wisdom, our founders understood that our nation could be God's people through the New Covenant of Jesus Christ, which is for "whosoever believes" and it is a better covenant than the Old Covenant (Hebrews 8:6). The USA as a covenant Christian nation is like a husband and wife making a covenant of their family to God. Israel shows us that God wants covenant nations.

Some think the USA is no longer a Christian nation. But consider Judah. Was Judah no longer a covenant nation to the LORD when King Manasseh and the people did so much evil? At least one person was faithful to God. Thus when King Josiah took reign, he soon saw the nation follow God.

That is where some people miss it. Are you no longer a Christian if you fall into sin? As long as you hold onto Jesus, which is holding onto covenant, you are a Christian. *For a just man falls seven times, and rises up again* (Proverbs 24:16).

Our country became a weak Christian nation by taking the Bible and Christian prayer out of schools, but the USA is a

Christian nation always by covenant. The remnant of true Americans who believe must unite and make a strong Christian nation now! Pastors must teach that America came from these secrets to success that we are learning.

The USA Exalts Jesus Christ

We have great optimism from the Jamestown Settlers' covenant. They brought the Bible with them and "had daily Common Prayer morning and evening, every Sunday, two sermons,"[4] with ministers who "followed the banner of the Cross".[5] If your school didn't censor it, you will recall that their first act was to pray, fast, plant a cross on the Virginia beach, and covenant America to God "to all generations".

Our covenant from 1607 says:

We do hereby dedicate this Land, and ourselves, to reach the People within these shores with the Gospel of Jesus Christ, and to raise up Godly generations after us, and with these generations take the Kingdom of God to all the earth. May this Covenant of Dedication remain to all generations, as long as this earth remains, and may this Land, along with England, be Evangelist to the World. May all who see this Cross, remember what we have done here, and may those who come here to inhabit join us in this Covenant...[6] (Jamestown Settlers, 1607)

The Pilgrims' covenant love for God also gives us hope. The Mayflower Compact reveals our country is God's nation:

IN THE NAME OF GOD, AMEN... Having undertaken for the Glory of God, and Advancement of the Christian Faith... Do by these Presents, solemnly and mutually, in the Presence of God and one another, covenant and combine ourselves together into a civil Body Politick... Anno Domini; 1620.[7]

The Puritans arrived in 1630. Famous John Winthrop wrote, *We are entered into covenant with Him for this work.*[8]

As Moses instructed Israel, our leaders John Hancock, George Washington, John Adams, and John Jay also taught to only acknowledge God's government. *There is no authority, civil or religious—there can be no legitimate government but what is administered by this Holy Ghost. There can be no salvation without it. All without it is rebellion and perdition, or in more orthodox words, damnation,*[9] said John Adams

The Library of Congress says, *Congress... held that God bound himself in an agreement with a nation and its people. This agreement stipulated that they "should be prosperous or afflicted, according as their general Obedience or Disobedience thereto appears...*[10]

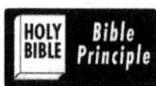

HOLY BIBLE **Bible Principle**

The USA's covenant with God is why God favors our nation.

And government *was convinced... the 'public prosperity' of a society depended on the vitality of its [Christian] religion. Nothing less than a 'spirit of universal reformation among all ranks and degrees of our citizens,' Congress declared to all, would 'make us a holy, that so we may be a happy people.'*[10]

Motivated to make disciples, our founders taught all children the Bible and Christian prayer in schools so both Christians and non-Christians could know God. In covenant George Washington assured Delaware Indian chiefs that the USA's schools were built on Christianity.

I am glad you have brought three of the children of your principal chiefs to be educated with us... You do well to wish to learn... above all, the religion of Jesus Christ. These will make you a greater and happier people than you are. Congress will do everything they can to assist you in this wise intention,[11] said Washington, our most famous president.

Americans made disciples of children with the Bible and Christian prayer in schools for 355 years (1607-1962) to keep covenant. Our Declaration of Independence is a covenant act that shows the USA serves God rather than man. The USA has some of the greatest Christian acts ever.

America is one of the pinnacles of Christianity, which is why we have led much of Christianity. The reformation produced the Bible in English and miraculously gathered mature Christians to form our covenant nation. The USA is much more than a nation of Christians, for even if only one person was in covenant, God honors our covenant. The good news is that I hear from people across America keeping our covenant daily. One person told me that their family named their apartment complex the "In God We Trust Building".

The Supreme Court tells us, *This is a Christian nation.*[12] Boldly the Pledge of Allegiance testifies that our country is a Christian Republic with the phrase, *to the Republic for which it stands, one nation under God.* Which God? The LORD.

Those who disagree are the people causing God's judgment because to say America is no longer a Christian nation is a covenant breaking act. Those who believe are in covenant—the true American believers. Even if some are unfaithful, it is important that you believe. Even though Judah killed their children and tolerated homosexual sin at times, the faithful remnant arose and followed God, which resulted in revival. If King Josiah had said Judah (Israel) was not a covenant nation, God would have destroyed them. But Josiah was part of the remnant who faithfully believed God.

Our founders and Israel saw others who didn't believe, but that didn't stop them. In the beginning just tens or hundreds of people claimed America for God. Look what their faith did!

It is unwise to listen to Obama and others who are not in our covenant. Their words have no meaning. David never paid attention to Goliath and Abraham did not listen to the Sodomites. The devil is the one that tempts people to doubt the things of God. We must never betray God and country by giving up America's foundation on Jesus Christ.

What about unbelievers in the USA? God's law applies to believers and unbelievers. *One ordinance shall be both for you of the congregation, and also for the foreigner that dwells*

43

with you (Numbers 15:15). The believer sanctifies the unbeliever (1 Cor. 7:14). By covenant Christian are in charge. As another proof the USA is a Christian nation, almost all political candidates say they are Christians even if they aren't.

An amazing point is that 11% of all the Christians on the earth live in the USA.[13] This is higher than every other country. The USA has only 4.4% of the total population of the world. Those calling themselves Christians greatly outnumber all others in our nation. More than seven out of ten identify as Christians. There are few Hindus, 0.7%, and few Muslims, 0.9%.[14] The large majority chooses Christianity even though not all have called on Jesus Christ to save their soul. The sin of political correctness to not offend unbelievers by hiding the truth that the USA is a Christian nation *offends God*; this has caused judgment as God commands that our loyalty is to Him.

We combine God and country to make the USA holy. The Declaration of Independence, Pledge of Allegiance, and Constitution do this. God is glorified in songs like *God Bless America, My Country 'Tis of Thee, America the Beautiful,* and our national anthem that says, *Praise the P'wer that has preserved and kept us... And this be our motto: "In God is our trust."*

HOLY BIBLE *Bible Principle*

Our founders show how a few people can make the strongest Christian nation.

Just as God and His mercy keeps your personal covenant with Him intact, He keeps the USA's covenant intact. God is faithful. I proclaim: *The LORD is the God of the USA and Americans are His people,* so I am in full covenant. I submit our country entirely to God continually. This is saying the USA is a Christian nation to all generations. Will you join me?

Today millions of Americans love God. If we do what our founders did, we will have a strong Christian nation. Will you and your church reclaim the USA for Jesus? Our founders were more mature Christians than those who state the USA isn't a Christian nation. They took our nation by spiritual force.

We need to remain faithful to God, for if no one holds fast to covenant, then Satan and evil people can destroy our country. It is the devil saying that our founders weren't Christians but deists. Our founders' acts prove they are Christians. Remember, if our founders sinned in some area, God is more gracious than we are. God honors David who sinned but repented. He never said David wasn't a believer.

Sadly, some Christians today criticize our founders. But have those dishonoring our founders risked their life for the USA to break free from tyranny to follow God? Do they say America belongs to Jesus Christ? Have they put the Bible in schools? Will they declare to our country their "abhorrence and detestation" of homosexual sin as George Washington did?[15] We are to hold fast to covenant and honor our founders.

HOLY BIBLE **Bible Principle**

God rewards covenant acts of loyalty.

Covenant Acts

Look at some of the USA's covenant acts that God blesses:

- The covenants (Jamestown Settlers, Pilgrims, Puritans...)
- The Revolution motto, "No king but King Jesus"
- George Washington reading the Holy Bible and praying in Jesus' name as the first act of Congress
- Teaching it is the duty of nations to serve God
- Americans declaring they obey God rather than man in the Declaration of Independence
- Singing "We trust in God: New England's God forever reigns" in the American Revolution song *Chester*
- The Constitution protecting our God-given rights
- All 50 states making Bible based laws for righteousness, such as outlawing gay sin and killing unborn children
- The Holy Bible and Christian Prayer in Schools for all children, Christian or non-Christian
- Government attending Christian churches in the Capital
- Our National Anthem saying, "In God is our trust"
- "This nation under God," affirmed Abraham Lincoln

- Our National Motto is "In God we trust"
- US currency saying, "In God we trust"
- Government *recognizes the Supreme Authority and Just Government of Almighty God,*[16] said Abraham Lincoln
- The National Day of Prayer, Christmas, and Thanksgiving supported by Federal law
- "One Nation Under God" in the Pledge of Allegiance

Re-affirming Covenant Is How to End Terrorism

We know how to stop losing the war on terror. Terrorism is defeated by: (1) Covenant acts that the LORD is the God of the USA and Americans are His people and (2) Our nation obeying the Bible. To protect our loved ones, declare *Jesus Christ is Lord of the USA* and choose Christian leaders. The *7 Bible Truths* are guaranteed to end terror, a curse from our national sins (Lev. 26:14-16). We proudly celebrate American culture of God and country. By saying the USA is a Christian nation, we ask God to protect His nation and He does.

Secret 3: Demand Our God-given Rights

Your rights come from God. The Declaration of Independence says, *all men are endowed by their Creator with certain unalienable rights, among these are life, liberty, and the pursuit of happiness.* This also gives you the right of property and conscience. No one, including government, can take away our rights because God gives our rights, not man (Acts 5:29).

HOLY BIBLE **Bible Principle**

You are created in the image of God and hold a noble rank in creation.

America's third secret to freedom is to demand our God-given rights, since man is made in the image of God (Genesis 1:27). John Adams said to pastors, *Let us hear the dignity of his nature, and the noble rank he holds among the works of God—that consenting to [tyranny] slavery is a sacrilegious breach of trust, as offensive in the sight of God as it is derogatory from our own honor or interest or happiness—and that God Almighty has promulgated from heaven liberty, peace, and good-will to man!*[17]

46

Your unalienable rights are to live for God, and include:

- **Life:** You have the right to life in all you do, beginning at conception. In Jesus is life, so this right is to follow Him. The Bible says, "In Him was life; and the life was the light of men" (John 1:4 KJV). "Life is the immediate gift of God, a right inherent by Nature [God's creation] in every individual and it begins in contemplation of law as soon as an infant is able to stir in the mother's womb" and "consists in the free use, enjoyment, and disposal of every man's acquisitions, without any control or diminution,"[18] explained scholar Sir William Blackstone.

- **Liberty:** Your right of liberty includes freedom to live your life for God as a Christian, not to live in sin. Jesus is the Author of Liberty and only He makes you free. Personal liberty "consists in the power of removing one's person to any place whatsoever without restraint, unless by due course of law," said Blackstone.[19] Americans reject tyranny because tyrants oppose God.

- **The Pursuit of happiness:** Your right to the pursuit of happiness is to do God's will because you are created in such a way that you can only be happy doing God's will. Psalm 144:15 says, "Happy is that people, whose God is the LORD!" The law of nature (the will of God) forbids doing things that are against another person's pursuit of happiness. Jesus commanded, "You shall love your neighbor as yourself" (Mark 12:31).

- **Property:** You have the right to property. This includes using your property to glorify God. Psalm 24:1 says, "The earth is the LORD's, and the fullness thereof". A person's right of private property "consists in the free use, enjoyment, and disposal of all his acquisitions, without any control or diminution, save only by the [Christian] laws of the land," explained Blackstone.[20]

47

- **Conscience:** Your right of conscience is the duty to obey your conscience before God in holiness (Acts 5:29). The Bible teaches that no one can force you to sin. A person who tries to force you to sin is evil.

Unalienable Rights Are a Non-negotiable

Boldly the "father of the Revolution," Samuel Adams, reminds us of our sacred duty to keep our rights, *The right to freedom being the gift of God Almighty...*[21] We should think like our founders. Abiding in Christ as free men and making disciples is higher living than just getting saved.

We have God-given rights to follow the LORD, not Satan-given rights to rebel against God in sin. People pushing for sin such as gay and abortion rights don't have rights from God. Our founders rejected these rights to sin from the devil.

We need every pastor to teach our God-given rights. *The clergy in all the colonies were bold and frequent in their pulpit enunciations of the great principles of civil and [Christian] religious liberty and in rebuking despotism and the evils of the day,* explained Robert Morris.[22]

Secret 4: Teach the Gospel of Jesus Christ

Our founders loved God with all their heart; they passionately believed and taught the Holy Bible. In 1 Corinthians 15:3-7, Paul summarizes the central part of the gospel, *Christ died for our sins according to the Scriptures; And that He was buried, and that He rose again the third day according to the Scriptures... After that, He was seen of above five hundred brethren at once... then of all the apostles.*

As Christians, we agree on the following core beliefs of the Gospel of Jesus Christ:

- **God** - God eternally exists in three Persons as Father, Son, and Holy Spirit. He is the one true God (Matthew 28:19, Isaiah 43:10-11, John 8:58).

- **God's Word is infallible** - The Holy Bible is our final authority in all matters of faith and practice (2 Timothy 3:16-17, 2 Peter 1:21, 1 Thessalonians 2:13).

- **The fall of man and salvation through Jesus Christ** - All have sinned, come short of the glory of God, and face the judgment of God. Each person individually is to call on Jesus Christ to be saved, for by grace we are saved through faith. Jesus Christ was born of a virgin and lived a perfect sinless life; He is the Lamb of God who takes away the sin of the world and died for our sins. He was buried and rose from the dead (Romans 3:23 & 6:23, John 1:29 & 3:16, Ephesians 2:8-9, Matthew 1:23, Hebrews 7:26, 1 Corinthians 15:4).

- **God commands us to love Him and to love one another** - The First Commandment is to "love the Lord your God with all your heart, and with all your soul, and with all your mind, and with all your strength." The Second Commandment is to "love your neighbor as yourself" (Mark 12:30-31).

- **Christians are to live holy lives** - God gives us the Holy Spirit so we can glorify Him in all we do (Romans 8:13-14, Galatians 5:22-23).

Secret 5: Teach Righteousness Exalts the USA

Wanting our nation to glorify God, both the colonial and American Revolution pastors taught, *Righteousness exalts a nation: but sin is a reproach to any people* (Proverbs 14:34). God is righteous; He is pro-life and for sexual purity of one man and one woman in a lifetime marriage.

Righteousness is the fifth secret to America's freedom. This is to: (1) Serve the LORD only—not to have any false gods; (2) Have the Holy Bible and Christian prayer in schools and government; (3) Be pro-life; (4) Have traditional marriage only; and (5) Other Biblical holy ways that God blesses.

Secret 6: Jesus Christ Leads the Government

The purpose of government is to serve Jesus Christ (Isaiah 9:6). Part of this is to secure our unalienable rights. God's fourth secret to America's blessings is government, schools, courts, police forces, and the military having their objective to glorify God.

Some think that church and state are to be kept separate, but the opposite is the truth. Our founders kept the state out of the church *not* the church out of the state. The water is to be out of the boat, but the boat is in the water. The real question is, "Does God require the USA to obey Him?" He says, "If we deny Him, He also will deny us" (2 Timothy 2:12). The First Commandment is to love God, so the devil is behind the lie of separation of church and state (Mark 12:30). Freedom and abundance came to the USA and Israel by serving God.

The USA Honors Christians

Joseph Story was appointed to the Supreme Court in 1811 by James Madison and wrote our Constitution's first extensive commentary; **Justice Joseph Story explained the First Amendment is for Christianity.** The First Amendment is not to approve of non-Christian beliefs as some in error say today. Law students studied Story's popular "Commentaries on the Constitution" from 1833 to 1905. It explains:

> *The real object of the [First] Amendment was, not to countenance [approve], much less to advance Mohammedanism, or Judaism, or infidelity [secularism], by prostrating Christianity, but to exclude all rivalry among Christian sects, and to prevent any national ecclesiastical establishment [denomination], which should give to an hierarchy the exclusive patronage of the national government.*[23]

In 1833 Chief Justice John Marshall affirmed Story's work as "an accurate commentary on our Constitution, formed in the spirit of the original text" that all statesmen should read.[24] The media, judges, and schools have lied about the First Amendment to use it against Christians by saying, "the Christian activity is a violation of church and state", Our founders prayed in Jesus' name, read the Bible in government, and wrote the Constitution. Laws against Christians and our conscience are illegal. **The First Amendment means:**

Congress [because its rights are limited] shall make no law respecting an establishment of [one Christian denomination] religion, or prohibiting the free exercise [of Christianity] thereof...

Christians wrote our Christian Constitution for Christians. It: (1) Begins with "blessings;" (2) Restricts Congress from making a law prohibiting the free exercise of Christianity in the First Amendment; (3) Includes "Sundays excepted" to honor the Lord in Article 1, Section 7; (4) Ends with "in the Year of our Lord" affirming Jesus Christ is Lord of the USA; and (5) Has Bible principles throughout. It is based on our Christian Declaration of Independence.

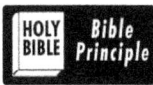

HOLY BIBLE *Bible Principle*

The First Amendment prohibits laws against Christians as the First Commandment is to love the LORD.

By our form of government, the Christian religion is the established religion; and all sects and denominations of Christians are placed upon the same equal footing, and are equally entitled to protection in their religious liberty,[25] said Justice Samuel Chase in the Maryland case Runkel v. Winemiller. George Washington appointed Chase to the Supreme Court.

Christians cause God's favor to the USA, not unbelievers. Our founders taught school children, "Almost all civil liberty...

51

owes its origin to the principles of the Christian religion."[26]

Secret 7: Christian Disciple Making in Government

Both the USA and Israel taught God's Word to the people because God asks for and blesses the government making disciples. This is America's fifth secret to have God's freedom and prosperity. We are not a state run church, but government is to support the church in disciple making.

Our founding fathers show us that all Christian denominations run the government with one focus to advance the Christian faith. God wants the church in charge not sinners. God's plan is that the church is in the driver's seat. But, the devil runs the parts not submitted to God.

To have Christianity in schools and for chaplains to pray in Jesus' name like our founders, the church must want government to glorify God. Our forefathers made disciples by forbidding homosexual and other sins in government. Thomas Jefferson, James Madison, and Americans had Christian church in the Capitol.[27]

The LORD Is the God of the USA

God's secrets of America give you favor too. Just reject all other gods and declare, *The LORD is my God and I am His.* Even if you have gone astray, remember that your Father runs to embrace all coming home to Him. Pray and He will take you in His arms and put the best robe on you. The prodigal son parable shows your Father's tender care. God loves you!

Now, will you join covenant by agreeing the LORD is the USA's God? This lets God know that you and the USA are on His side, which means liberty, prosperity, and the defeat of our enemies, including terrorism. Every person and church who agrees brings healing to our land, but those not making the LORD our God cause His judgment.

Next, we learn what it means to find and be near to God.

✝ *Prayer*

*Father, You, LORD, are the God of the USA
and Americans are Your people. In Jesus' name. Amen.*

✓ *Summary and Reflection Questions*

America is unlike other nations. The secrets in this chapter plus all the *7 Bible Truths* are how to make the USA great again. To get out of our current danger, we must do what our founders did. As Christians, we must consecrate our nation entirely to God. The USA is a Christian nation to all generations!

1. *What do you gain by re-affirming: The LORD is the God of the USA and Americans are His people?*
2. *Why must we declare the USA is a Christian nation?*
3. *Why do we call for Christian religious liberty only?*
4. *Explain each of your God-given rights.*

4
Second Truth—Seek... Find God

George Washington seeking the LORD God.

*"They entered into a covenant to seek the LORD God
of their fathers with all their heart and with all their soul;"*
2 Chronicles 15:12 KJV

George Washington kneels in desperation searching for answers. As commander in chief, all he could do at this point was seek the true Commander in Chief, our Lord. His men were sick, hungry, and cold. He had sought help earnestly from men, but it wasn't enough. So as he often did, he knelt to seek God's help at Valley Forge.

What is the next timely step to deliver us from our troubles, including national security risks, political problems, helplessness, and a potential economic collapse? *The Second Bible Truth is seeking God with all your heart and all your soul guarantees that He will save the USA and bless You. When we seek God we find Him and we are near to Him.*

Second Bible Truth to end God's judgment *2 Chron. 15:12, Matt. 7:7*	**Seek God with all your heart and all your soul** *Why? To find and be near to God.*

Bible Blessings: How to Guarantee God Will Save the USA and Bless You

Humbling Ourselves Before the LORD

To seek God is to humble ourselves before Him to find His help. As a personal example, one time as I sought God for His immediate direction in my life, I wrestled with decisions that would impact my future. I put all things aside to find God's help. Instead of pursuing doors I thought would be best, I sought God until He opened doors for me. I prayed daily to do God's will for my life and He revealed to me which doors to go through. As a result, a situation that I previously saw as insurmountable was now overcome. By humbling ourselves we find God's help to be free of the dangers we face.

When Judah humbled themselves to make covenant in Asa's time, the people were happy to seek God and end their problems. *Judah rejoiced at the oath: for they had sworn with all their heart, and sought Him with their whole desire; and He was found of them: and the LORD gave them rest round about* (2 Chronicles 15:15). The reason Judah was not destroyed in Josiah's life is because God saw Josiah humble himself (2 Kings 22:19). Moses had great grace from God as he was the most humble person on earth (Numbers 12:3).

We are to seek God with all our heart and all our soul for the USA (Deuteronomy 4:29). Our heart is our inner man and we seek God from deep within. Our soul is our mind, will, and emotions. So we: (1) Seek God with all our thoughts and intellect, (2) Search for His will, and (3) Seek Him with all our love for Him. Even in fear or despair we turn to God for help instead of other people or something else for comfort.

Jesus promises, *Ask, and it shall be given you; seek, and ye shall find; knock, and it shall be opened unto you* (Matthew

55

7:7 KJV). Our churches must seek Him for the USA. We are desperate to find God's help to end His judgment so everything will be well.

To put God first can be to not answer the phone or read our text messages until we have found Him. Moses often "fell upon his face" to seek God with his whole being when in need and God immediately answered him. With all the sins in the USA, our whole nation should fall on our faces and seek God for immediate deliverance. Like Moses, our nation is to seek God with a deep hunger and as one who wants to find Him (Numbers 16:22).

We have confidence God hears us for every Christian is accepted with Him. By shedding His blood for you on the cross, Jesus makes you holy, without blemish, blameless, and above reproach, no matter what your sins have been. He presents you faultless with exceeding joy. So have faith that your prayers are answered when you ask according to God's Word (Ephesians 1:6 & 5:22, Col. 1:22, Jude 1:24, 1 John 1:7).

When we ask God for His help, He lovingly helps us with His hand for our needs, including to deliver us from our enemies, foreign and domestic.

God Rewards You for Seeking Him

We are to seek God for our personal lives to be right with Him too. He wants us to walk with Him and find His counsel and miraculous help in all that we do.

God is interested in each of us. He wants us to fellowship with Him, so He kindly invites us to know Him. David said, *Your face, LORD, will I seek* (Psalm 27:8). This is knowing God for who He is and not just for what He can do for us. This is another level of seeking God. We are created to worship God in reverence and to enjoy Him as our best friend.

He answers us when we pray in faith. He says, *Delight yourself also in the LORD; and He shall give you the desires of your heart* (Psalm 37:4). When you seek God:

- **You find God:** *You shall find Him, if you seek Him with all your heart and with all your soul.* (Deuteronomy 4:29)
- **The LORD helps you:** *For You, LORD, have not forsaken those who seek You. (Psalm 9:10 KJV)*
- **God rewards you:** *But without faith it is impossible to please Him, for he who comes to God must believe that He is, and that He is a rewarder of those who diligently seek Him. (Hebrews 11:6 KJV)*
- **You prosper:** *As long as he sought the LORD, God made him to prosper. (2 Chronicles 26:5 KJV)*
- **You have all you need:** *They that seek the LORD shall not want any good thing. (Psalm 34:10 KJV)*
- **You do God's work:** *Now set your heart and your soul to seek the LORD your God; arise therefore, and build. (2 Chronicles 12:14 KJV)*
- **You have life:** *Your heart shall live* that seek God. (Psalm 69:32 KJV)* *The word "live" means to have life, live prosperously, and to be restored to health.
- **You avoid evil:** *He did evil, because he prepared not his heart to seek the LORD. (2 Chronicles 12:14 KJV)*
- **You understand all things:** *They that seek the LORD understand all things. (Proverbs 28:5 KJV)*

How to Find God in Your Personal Life

Here are five Biblical principles to help find God. First, each of us must make the decision to live following God. The Bible says, *Submit yourselves therefore to God. Resist the devil, and he will flee from you* (James 4:7). Remove anything unholy in your life. Put off ungodly conversations, thoughts, shows, art, and

HOLY BIBLE **Bible Principle**

What does God want you to seek Him for?

anything that displeases God. Instead, seek the things above where Christ is seated (Colossians 3:1-3). The Holy Spirit gives you self control, so think thoughts of love for God and others. Then resist the devil. A good prayer is, *Father, You*

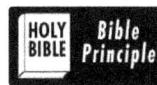

57

are holy. I want to be holy. Fill me with Your Holy Spirit so my life glorifies You. In Jesus' name. Amen.

Second, pray God's Word. Jesus promises that if we abide in Him and His words abide in us, we shall ask what we will and it shall be done unto us (John 15:7).

The third thing to do is to have faith that God will answer you. Christians walk by faith, not by sight (2 Corinthians 5:7). To live by faith is to live by God's Word. We can pray, *Father, great is Your faithfulness. I walk by Your Word. Thank You for answering me. In Jesus' name. Amen.*

A secret that God graciously revealed to me is to never stop seeking Him until I find Him, whether it takes a moment or two hours. God is faithful to answer us when we believe that He will help us right now. If we expect God's immediate help, we see answers and miracles quickly (Mark 11:23-24).

Fourth, seek God continually, not just when in trouble. God promises, *He that dwells in the secret place of the Most High shall abide under the shadow of the Almighty* (Psalm 91:1). *Evening, and morning, and at noon, will I pray, and cry aloud: and He shall hear my voice* (Psalm 55:17 KJV).

Fifth, let God know that you are willing to do His will. When you let go of your will, you can find God's will. God says, "I have found David... a man after Mine own heart, which shall fulfill all My will" (Acts 13:22). These Biblical points help all your prayers be answered, even immediately.

So I can draw near to God quickly and have deeper fellowship with Him, in the morning, after telling God I love Him and blessing Him, I pray the four steps of 2 Chronicles 7:14. *Father, I humble myself, pray, seek Your face, and turn from my wicked ways. In Jesus' name. Amen.*

When you make a decision, seek God first. He will lead you. If you don't know what to do, you can pray as a commitment prayer Proverbs 3:5-6. *Father, I trust in You with all my heart regarding ___. I lean not on my own understanding about this. I acknowledge You in this, and I thank You for directing my paths. In Jesus' name. Amen.*

Anything we seek God's will for can be placed in that blank line. If you are seeking God about where to serve Him, You would insert, "the perfect place You have for me to serve You," in the blank line. God will direct your steps since this is His promise.

Jesus continually sought God to know His will, always finding and doing the Father's will. Jesus did this when He had to lay down His life for us at Calvary. Since Jesus is also a man, He didn't want to feel the immense suffering of the cross because He would be scourged, mocked, and painfully crucified for our sins.

With fear and great depression, knowing how much He would suffer for us to be forgiven of our sins, He

You find God when you seek Him with all your heart and all your soul.

fell down in Gethsemane and asked God if there was another way to save you and me. Since there was no other way, Jesus arose with courage and endured the cross for us. Hopefully you realize that "nothing could stop Jesus from loving you," as I say in my sermon, "Jesus Loved You on the Cross."

A popular hymn, "Sweet Hour of Prayer," encourages us to spend time with God in prayer, *That calls me from a world of care, and bids me at my Father's throne. Make all my wants and wishes known...* Prayer strengthens your life.

If you need God's peace, His power, the right words to comfort someone, or assistance with what you are doing, just ask Him. He promises to *supply all your needs according to His riches in glory by Christ Jesus* (Philippians 4:19).

One day I had a three hundred mile drive to make, but because of my busy schedule at USA Christian Church I could not leave until 8 p.m. After driving thirty minutes I was tired and I didn't think I could go further. But I prayed in faith for God to help me and to safely get me to my destination, expecting Him to answer me immediately. Miraculously in just minutes I felt God's strength and grace. I was awake and a five hour drive seemed like it was only two hours!

How to Seek God for the USA

When was the last time you heard someone say: "What does the Bible say to do to get out of the trillions of debt?" or "Does God want us to fight this war?" or "Would God want us to violate our consciences with government paid abortions?" or "How can our public schools exalt Jesus Christ?"

The church's responsibility is to seek God for our nation to do His will, but many are waiting for ungodly politicians to decide to follow God. We are to repent of hopelessly waiting for politicians, that God uses in judgment, to decide what is right and wrong. High taxes and foreigners taking our jobs came from the church not seeking God for our country. But by seeking God and doing His will, jobs will come back and the dollar won't collapse from the debt. By seeking God, the USA prospers (2 Chronicles 7:13-14, Deuteronomy 28:15-21).

I was praying in June 2008 and God revealed to me an amazing truth that will turn things around for us. I learned our nation's abortions had reached heaven. Therefore, God was giving the USA people to vote for who would destroy it.

At first I didn't fully understand what God was telling me. But with continued prayer and searching God's Word, I understood much of the judgment through corrupt politicians was because the land was polluted with blood. Since the Bible affirms politicians who hate Americans result from shedding innocent blood and other sins, it was true (Psalm 106:37-42). Some of this destruction we read earlier with censorship on free speech, persecuting Christians, reckless spending, and attacking our Constitution and Declaration of Independence.

As I continued to seek God on how to save our nation, I learned of God's graciousness. He desires mercy for us instead of destroying our country. To save the USA we are to re-affirm covenant with these *7 Bible Truths*.

Seeking God daily is a commitment. After I made the decision to help our nation live for Jesus, I could have stopped many times and done something else. But I know that strengthening the USA in Christ is God's priority for me. If Paul didn't seek God daily, then he would have done other things instead of building up Christians. A question that each of us can prayerfully ask is, *What would I do if I were to seek first the Kingdom of God and His righteousness in my life and for the USA?* (Matthew 6:33)

Our nation seeking God is especially important. When Israel suffered a famine, King David sought God and learned what sin caused judgment. *The LORD answered, It is for Saul, and for his bloody house, because he slew the Gibeonites* (2 Samuel 21:1 KJV). The Gibeonites lived in Israel's promised land and were to be destroyed. But they lied to Israel and Israel made a treaty because they didn't seek God (Joshua 9). Then, when Saul went against Joshua's words, God judged them. But David found the answer to stop judgment in prayer!

I hope that you are optimistic because doing these *Bible Truths* will bring back jobs for Americans and end wars. Following God's blueprint will save millions of souls, heal marriages, free our nation from communist threats, protect animals, and have Christians honored again.

To help our nation seek the LORD, here are some questions that we and our churches can prayerfully ask:

- Will this act bring God's blessings or judgment?
- Does this decision bring Americans closer to God?
- How can the USA's sins be forgiven?
- Why does God forbid other gods in the USA?
- If we do this will more go to Heaven or hell?
- What qualifications does God have for leaders?
- How does the Bible say to remove tyranny?
- Will this choice make us more heavenly or worldly?
- What national sins can we repent of?

God has the answers we are searching for. But have you noticed those who do not believe God will save our nation focus on the problems, not on our all powerful God? If you have done this, ask God to forgive you. Our founders and Moses believed God would help them and God did. So by faith we believe that God is removing everything against Him from the USA and young Americans will live as faithful Christians. God will reward our work (2 Chronicles 15:7).

Some think it's a fulfillment of prophecy to remove the USA so they no longer teach all things Jesus commanded, including nationwide repentance. But the church cannot take our hand off the plow. We are certain we are being judged, but no one knows one hundred percent that Jesus is coming back this moment. While we long for Jesus to return now, we can't stop making disciples.

HOLY BIBLE *Bible Principle*

We are to seek God and make disciples of the USA until Jesus' returns, not to use the rapture or the tribulation as an excuse to stop.

Prophecy is interesting, but when was the last time you heard those over-emphasizing prophecy say, "to stop God's judgment the USA must renounce Islam, Mormonism, and all false gods" or "most of the USA's problems are God's discipline for the people supporting pagan leaders"? When people don't understand that the loss of freedoms is from angering God, they don't say repent or fight for liberty. If you have done this, ask God to forgive you.

Others think they need to hide during the tribulation instead of calling on God to save us. And some just wait idle for Jesus' return. The truth is whether we believe Christians will be raptured or go through the tribulation, God doesn't say to stop teaching Americans to live to glorify Him.

There is hope. God answers prayer that is based on His Word and prayed in faith. He does promise to heal our land if we turn from our wicked ways (2 Chronicles 7:14). That's why we must share these *7 Bible Truths*.

Faithfully serving Jesus Christ helps us to be ready for His return. He said that "repentance and remission of sins should be preached in His name" to the USA (Luke 24:47). This is a top priority, so listen to pastors who teach repentance.

Turn Away from Those Not Seeking God

Even as we desire God, there may still be those who don't renounce strange gods or their pursuit of the world, which perpetuates God's wrath. King Asa realized this Scriptural revelation. The Old Testament says, "whosoever would not seek the LORD God of Israel should be put to death, whether small or great, whether man or woman" (2 Chronicles 15:13 KJV). Moses and King Josiah also put to death those who wouldn't follow God (Exodus 32:26-28, 2 Kings 23:4-25). **For us, we don't kill people, but we "turn away" from those responsible for our nation's judgment** (2 Timothy 3:5).

To "turn away" means to identify and then shun or avoid those who don't seek the LORD for the USA since God says they are the ones causing our troubles. We notice that they don't really want to do God's will. While we share that Jesus died on the cross to forgive our sins to those living in darkness, the Bible teaches that we are to turn away from ungodly people, politicians, businesses, and media. God is not with them, so we don't gain any benefit by listening to them.

Remember, the Bible says more spoiling of the USA's money and terrorism came from Congress, the National Prayer Breakfast, and the National Cathedral praying with Buddhists, Muslims, and other false ways,[2] provoking God. Instead of being silent about spiritual adultery, be faithful to seek the LORD only. Our founders wouldn't listen to those seeking strange gods (2 Kings 17:15-20, Leviticus 26:14-16).

God is with those who are with Him, so Congress in 1777 declared, *That it may please GOD, through the Merits of Jesus Christ... to afford his Blessing on the Governments of these States... to prosper the Means of [Christian] Religion for the promotion and enlargement of that Kingdom which consists 'in Righteousness, Peace and Joy in the Holy Ghost.[3]*

Our founders only appointed Christian chaplains to seek God. That is why the House Judiciary Committee, *resolved, that the daily sessions of this body be opened with prayer and that... the [Christian] ministers of the Gospel... are hereby requested to attend and alternately perform this solemn duty.[4]*

Since the answer to be free of high taxes and our nation being shamed is to seek and obey God as a nation, pray to the LORD only. This makes the USA a safer and stronger place (2 Kings 17:15-20, Deuteronomy 28:29, Ezekiel 16:37).

Those Who Seek God Are On His Side

George Washington and his men made it through that difficult winter in Valley Forge defending our freedom because he humbled himself before the true Commander in Chief and found Him. God faithfully answered his prayer. When spring arrived, although the army was weakened, they were able to claim a resounding victory! Eventually God gave us complete victory and independence since Americans kept seeking Him with all their heart and soul.

Seeking God looks like George Washington pleading for God's help to defeat a stronger army. It looks like King Josiah tearing his clothes and weeping when he hears God's words and his eyes open, seeing the sins of the people. It looks like American pastors praying in Jesus' name for government, schools, courts, and the military.

It also looks like those joining in the nationwide prayer and fasting on Wednesdays to heal our land that I am hosting,[5] to have a Christian government, and our nation repenting of everything against Jesus Christ (Luke 11:2, 1 John 3:8).

Our founders trusted in God and He kept the USA safe from enemies, foreign and domestic. The Bible says, *Put not your trust in princes, nor in the son of man, in whom there is no help* and *except the LORD guards the city, the watchman keeps watch in vain* (Psalm 146:3, Psalm 127:1).

Now, it is our turn to be faithfully known for praying, *In God We Trust.* The USA's hope is God! We are to keep seeking God until we find Him.

If you haven't been seeking Him, I encourage you to start now. He wants to hear from you. His grace welcomes you!

Will you turn to God with all your heart and soul? If so, you are on His side. Then if you are on God's side, you can say, *The LORD is on my side; I will not fear: what can man do unto me?* (Psalm 118:6). Have faith! He always rewards the USA for seeking Him. Victory and miracles happen!

The next *Bible Truth* reveals how to do God's will.

✝ *Prayer*

Here is a prayer to seek God as a nation:

Father,

Americans love You—You are the USA's God and we are Your people. With all our heart and soul, we seek You to:

- *Mercifully end Your judgment.*
- *Lead our country. The USA submits to You.*
- *Give us Christian leaders who fear You for school boards, city, state, and federal government.*
- *Lead Americans not into temptation. Deliver the USA from evil (everything against You).*
- *Teach us if __ will make our nation holy, or unholy.*
- *Show Americans what Your Word says about __.*
- *We trust in You to protect the USA from all enemies foreign and domestic.*

Americans thank and praise You. In Jesus' name. Amen.

✓ *Summary and Reflection Questions*

By seeking God, we find Him and are close to Him. To get out of our troubles, we are to ask God what He wants us to do in our lives and in our Christian republic. Our churches seeking God to end our nation's judgment will stop the spoiling of our country's wealth, give better jobs for Americans, end wars, and cause our nation to have Christian character. God cares for us and wants to help us.

1. *Why is it urgent for the USA to humble ourselves and seek God?*

2. *How can you be like King Asa and King Josiah in seeking God with all your heart and all your soul? What are some things you will do?*

3. *How can your church seek God for the USA to end our national crisis? In what ways? How often?*

5

Third Truth—Live the Bible Way

"To keep His commandments... with all his heart, and with all his soul, to perform the words of the covenant which are written in this book." 2 Chronicles 34:31 KJV

Jesus Christ is the Word of God. This is an important reason why we stand in awe of God's Word. God says, *In the beginning was the Word, and the Word was with God, and the Word was God* and *His name is called The Word of God* (John 1:1, Revelation 19:13 KJV).

When King Josiah and Judah found the Word of God that their fathers lost, the people followed God's Word. Many in Judah had forsaken the one true God, killed their children, and turned away from God with homosexuality and the occult, but the nation made covenant *to follow the LORD, to keep His commandments and His testimonies and His statutes* (2 Chronicles 34). Following God solved their problems. Like Judah found the book of the law, we are discovering from God's Word these *7 Bible Truths* that end our nation's crisis.

Third Bible Truth to end God's judgment Luke 6:47-49, 2 Chron. 34:31	Obey the Holy Bible with all your heart and all your soul *Why? To do God's will.*

Bible Blessings: How to Guarantee God Will Save the USA and Bless You

The Third Bible Truth is obedience to the Word of God guarantees that God will save the USA and bless you because this is doing His will. To obey the LORD goes with the *Second Bible Truth* to seek and find Him, since part of seeking God is to learn what He says. This is living the Bible way. Since we love God, we obey Him.

All the judgments, and the fear many have, come to an end by following the Bible and re-affirming covenant with these *7 Bible Truths*. God, mercifully, is giving us a way out. We have great hope by doing His will.

Both our personal and nation's relationship with God is by His Word. To find God's will, pray: *What does the Bible say about this?* Then find in Scripture what a Christian is to do. We are on God's side when we keep His Word (John 15:14).

The Bible is the Secret to Remarkable Blessings

God gives us incomparable blessings when we observe and do what He says. God gave the USA the Deuteronomy 28 blessings before and He wants to do this now. He set America high above all nations, made the USA blessed in the city and in the field, and blessed American children, produce, and animals. He lovingly blessed the USA coming and going. He defeated America's enemies, commanded the blessing in all we do, and set Americans as a holy people to Himself.

But there is more... God made Americans plenteous in everything, prospered the USA financially—by lending to others not borrowing, and made us the head not the tail. Keeping God's Word makes the USA great. Your greatest blessings also come from the Bible. He tells you how to live the best way possible now and to be rewarded in Heaven.

I want to share seven blessings that God's Word gives you personally. First, you grow closer to God by His Word (Psalm 119). Second, the Word of God gives you life (Matthew 4:4). The third important benefit is having what you ask of God, since you ask according to His will (1 John 5:15, John 15:7).

Wisdom is the fourth amazing blessing (Proverbs 1). The fifth benefit is keeping God's Word gives you health (Exodus 15:26, Proverbs 4:20-22). The sixth benefit is having a true Christian home serving God (Joshua 24:15). The seventh blessing is strong faith, for *Faith comes by hearing, and hearing by the word of God* (Romans 10:17).

What Makes the Bible the #1 Best Seller?

Why did God give us the Bible? God preserves His Word to all generations so we can know Him and walk with Him as our Lawgiver, live in happiness, and be safe from harm. We learn the eternal mind and counsel of God when we read God's Word. The Bible is unique as it does not have human origin and it is the absolute final authority for us and our nation. That is why the Holy Bible is the top selling book in history and quoted by our respected founders.

God says to love one another, be honest, for families to stay together, forgive one another, believe that He will provide for us, live righteously, and how to be saved from the wrath to come. Is there anything unjust in the Bible? Is there anything in God's Word that doesn't help us live like Jesus?

My most valuable possession is my Bible. By God's Word, I know God and have everything I need. Here are ten keys why the Bible is of greater worth than every other book:

- **The Holy Bible is God's Word** from Genesis to Revelation - *All Scripture is given by inspiration of God (2 Timothy 3:16 KJV); For the prophecy came not in old time by the will of man: but holy men of God spake as they were moved by the Holy Ghost (2 Peter 1:21 KJV).*
- **The Word of God is eternal** - *Forever, O LORD, Your word is settled in heaven... every one of Your righteous judgments endures forever (Psalm 119:89 & 160).*

- **The Word of God cannot be broken** - *The Scripture cannot be broken (John 10:35 KJV).*
- **The Bible is true** - *Your Word is true from the beginning (Psalm 119:160).*
- **Scripture defeats the devil** - *Young men, because ye are strong, and the word of God abideth in you, and ye have overcome the wicked one (1 John 2:14 KJV).*
- **The Word of God protects you and the USA** - *His truth shall be your shield and buckler (Psalm 91:4).*
- **The Bible is living and powerful** - *For the word of God is living and powerful, and sharper than any two-edged sword, piercing even to the division of soul and spirit, and of joints and marrow, and is a discerner of the thoughts and intents of the heart (Hebrews 4:12 KJV).*
- **The Holy Bible is pure** - *The words of the LORD are pure words: as silver tried in a furnace of earth, purified seven times (Psalm 12:6 KJV).*
- **The Word of God will outlast the earth** - *For verily I say unto you, Till heaven and earth pass, one jot or one tittle shall in no wise pass from the law, till all be fulfilled (Matthew 5:18 KJV).*
- **God's Word makes you and America prosperous** - *This book of the law shall not depart out of your mouth; but you shall meditate in it day and night, that you may observe to do according to all that is written in it: for then you shall make your way prosperous, and then you shall have good success (Joshua 1:8).*

Jesus Christ accepted the authority of the Word of God and He quoted Scripture to defeat Satan. We also resist the devil by using the Bible. The devil knows that Scripture is the absolute authority, so when we speak and do God's Word the devil is defeated every time (Matthew 4:3-11). By the name of Jesus, the Word of God, and Jesus' blood, God gives Christians power over the devil.

Scripture is without error; every word is true. Every coma (i.e., jot) and dot (i.e., tittle) is true.

The LORD Is Our Lawgiver

To end our judgment, we must know the Bible is God's revealed law. It is our duty to observe the Word of our Creator or we face consequences. *The doctrines thus delivered we call the revealed or divine law, and they are to be found only in the Holy Scriptures,*[1] taught legal scholar Sir William Blackstone. Who makes our laws? Our founders practiced *the LORD is our Lawgiver* (Isaiah 33:22) and our laws are from Scripture. With wisdom they made Christian laws and expect us to keep them, including to honor God by traditional marriage. The Bible is the bedrock of the USA's legal system.

The Supreme Court affirmed, *It is well known that for our present form of government we are greatly indebted to his [Justice James Wilson's] exertions and influence... he states that profaneness and blasphemy [of God] are offences punishable by fine and imprisonment, and that Christianity is part of the common law.*[2] Wilson signed both the Declaration of Independence and the Constitution; George Washington appointed him to the original Supreme Court.

Human law must rest its authority, ultimately, upon the authority of that law, which is divine,[3] taught Justice Wilson, as the first law professor at the University of Pennsylvania.

We need Christian judges. Examples of judges that God approves of are Justices John Jay, James Wilson, and Joseph Story. But to have judges with God's wisdom we must choose Christian leaders who believe God is our Lawgiver. This requires pastors nationwide to call for a Christian government.

Since God is a covenant God, He asks us to have our government in covenant with Him (Isaiah 9:6 & 33:22). This means to choose leaders who are in covenant. Perhaps, the primary metric of the maturity of the USA in Christ is how strong is our *covenant Christian nation government*. This is a government that follows the *7 Bible Truths* and God blesses.

Why haven't we had a strong Christian government like our founders? The reasons are:

1. Pastors stopped teaching to vote for Christians only.
2. People voted for ungodly candidates.

Some amazing benefits of a Christian government are we have God-given rights, Christians honored, Christian laws, better jobs, a wiser nation, and freedom—like the America we love. A secret our founders knew is that elections are about pleasing God. For pastors to teach on politics is more than to say to vote for *family values* which has included unbelievers. It is to choose Christians who make laws based on the Bible.

Surprisingly, I saw a popular minister boast of not getting involved in politics, but pulpits silent on politics cause political corruption. Without pastors teaching how God says to vote, then people generally decide based on the media. But the media isn't giving God's counsel. Conservative media said the only way to replace Obama was to vote for Mormon Romney in 2012. Liberal media in 2008 shared Obama was messiah-like. Deception happens when pastors are silent.

To Fear God is the True Meaning of Presidential

The media also tries to tell us if a candidate is presidential or not and if they know foreign policy or not. But according to what definition? God's definition of presidential is to *fear God* and the best foreign policy is to have God's protection and favor. He does care about leaders and gives these instructions:

- *You shall provide out of all the people able men, such as fear God, men of truth, hating covetousness; and place such over them, to be rulers* (Exodus 18:21).
- *Be ye not unequally yoked together with unbelievers: for what fellowship has righteousness with unrighteous-ness?... Therefore come out from among them... and I will receive you...* (2 Corinthians 6:14-18 KJV)
- *He who leads as he that serves"* (Luke 22:26).
- *In the image of God He created him* (Genesis 1:27).
- *Proclaim liberty throughout all the land unto all the inhabitants thereof* (Leviticus 25:10 KJV).

We have hope of our land healing and God's judgment ending by each of us pledging to choose representatives from school boards to president who meet God's requirements for leaders. Our Lawmaker says to choose leaders based on five qualities and our founding fathers fulfilled these requirements.

The Bible's Five Requirements for Leaders

1. Able Christians Who Fear God *Ex. 18:21, 2 Cor. 6:14-18*
- They know the LORD is our Lawgiver, Judge, and King, so they obey the Holy Bible (Isaiah 33:22).
- Their goal is the true American Dream of advancing the Kingdom of our Lord Jesus Christ.
- Obeying God, they are pro-life and for traditional marriage only, and call for schools to have the Bible and Christian prayer (Matt. 5:21, 2 Peter 2:6, Is. 59:21).
- As Jesus Christ serves the church, they serve Americans (Luke 22:26).
- They believe that our national security is first *In God We Trust (*Mark 12:31, Psalm 121:1 & 146:3-5).
- They have a Biblical view of the USA's war policy, which is defensive (just cause) non-aggressive wars. If in war, they call to quickly win the war.

2. Call for Christian Religious Liberty *Mark 12:30, Gal. 5:1*
- Obeying God, they boldly stand up to have Christian religious liberty throughout the USA (Matthew 4:10).
- They understand that the Constitution was written by Christians to protect Christians to serve the LORD.

3. Insist to Have God-given Rights *Genesis 1:27, Acts 5:29*
- Since our rights are endowed by our Creator and can never be surrendered, they affirm our Biblical rights.
- They are known for defending our unalienable rights of life, liberty, the pursuit of happiness, property, and conscience.

4. Truthful *Exodus 18:21*
- They are known for honesty not lying.
- They condemn all unconstitutional acts, so they don't limit our rights, but they limit government's power.

5. Hate Covetousness *Exodus 8:21*
- They refuse to take what belongs to *We the People.*
- With verifiable histories, they prove that they are effective at eliminating unjust taxes and cutting debts.
- As the Bible teaches, they promote self-government.

Five Mistakes Voters Make that Grieve God

God is grieved if we don't follow His voting requirements. How can God be pleased if people vote for those who: (1) Don't obey God; (2) Persecute Christians; (3) Are tyrants who oppress people; (4) Lie; and (5) Raise taxes? God is good. We know choosing evil grieves the Holy Spirit.

Every church must teach God's leadership requirements so we have representatives who are on the LORD's side. On my website is the *American Christian Voting Guide*™ that shows who best meets God's requirements in elections.[4]

John Jay said, *it is the duty... of our Christian nation to select and prefer Christians for [our] rulers.*[5] As they used to do, schools need to teach how to choose Christian leaders:

> *It is alleged by men of loose principles, or defective views of the subject, that [Christian] religion and morality are not necessary or important qualifications for political stations. But the Scriptures ... direct that rulers should be men who rule in the fear of God, able men, such as fear God, men of truth, hating covetousness... [Exodus 18:21]*[6]

> *When you become entitled to exercise the right of voting for public officers, let it be impressed on your mind that God commands you to choose for rulers, 'just men who will rule in the fear of God.' [2 Samuel 23:3] The preservation of government depends on the faithful discharge of this Duty...*[7]

School children also learned the dangers of voting for the ungodly, *If the citizens neglect their Duty and place unprincipled men in office, the government will soon be corrupted; laws will be made, not for the public good so much as for selfish or local purposes; corrupt or incompetent men will be appointed to execute the Laws; the public revenues will be squandered on unworthy men; and the rights of the citizen will be violated or disregarded. If government fails to secure public prosperity and happiness, it must be because the citizens neglect the Divine Commands, and elect bad men to make and administer the Laws.*[7]

Important Reasons to Have Christians Leaders

More benefits and reasons for a Christian government are:

- God commands it
- To welcome Jesus Christ
- We keep covenant with God
- To have the Kingdom of God
- God blesses us rather than judges us
- Voting for non-Christians causes Christian persecution
- Without Christian leaders we have unholy laws
- Evil men cause the country to go the wrong direction

To vote for non-Christians is to reject Jesus Christ, since an unbeliever is not part of the Body of Christ. The people voting for the ungodly choose Satan to rule over them instead of God since the ungodly don't belong to God. The heathen are the children of the devil (John 8:44, 1 John 3:10). It is also to turn away from the Kingdom of God, since God's enemies are of the power of darkness, not Jesus' Kingdom (Colossians 1:13). This is a great sin that should convict our consciences so we turn away from ungodly people in politics.

Most of the problems we face come from ungodly leaders. God's enemies prevail when we vote for non-Christians. If we choose worldly leaders, we "help the ungodly". That is unwise for we know it provokes God to wrath. *Should you help the ungodly, and love them that hate the LORD? therefore is wrath upon you from before the LORD* (2 Chronicles 19:2). John Jay co-authored the Federalist Papers and he believed this verse applied to voting.[8] Jay became a ministry president and worked for God's Word to abound throughout our nation.

God says, *whoever therefore will be a friend of the world is the enemy of God* (James 4:4). To be enamored with ungodly but popular people in politics is to walk after the sinful nature not the Spirit. *Love not the world, neither the things that are in the world. If any man love the world, the love of the Father is not in him* (1 John 2:16).

If we vote for someone who doesn't fear God, then not only are we voting for God's enemies, but we become God's enemy too. This is part of God's Word that some have forgotten. Overlooking this caused the USA's well being to be at stake. So let's be God's friend and vote for those in Christ.

Others vote on how someone looks on the outside, but God says, *Do not look at his appearance or at his physical stature, because I have refused him. For the LORD does not see as man sees; for man looks at the outward appearance, but the LORD looks at the heart* (1 Samuel 16:7).

Political Judgments

There are terrible consequences for choosing people who don't fear God as leaders. Israel was destroyed by Egypt when they turned to Egypt for help instead of God. The troubles are:

1. God's wrath *2 Chronicles 19:2*
2. Being cursed - *Blessed is the man that walks not in the counsel of the ungodly... the ungodly shall not stand in the judgment, nor sinners in the congregation of the righteous... the way of the ungodly shall perish. Psalm 1:1 & 5-6*
3. God uses the wicked in judgment *Ezekiel 23, Romans 1:28*
4. Turning away from sonship with God - *Come out from among them, and be ye separate... touch not the unclean thing; and I will receive you. And will be a Father unto you, and ye shall be my sons and daughters. 2 Corinthians 6:17-18 KJV*

Christian leaders will end the persecution of Christians and heal our land, so we must vote for Christians. From 2008 to present, several popular ministers have misled the church by teaching that it is okay to vote for worldly people, which I discuss in a later chapter. This grieves God and quenches the Spirit. Let's look at the correlation in supporting God's enemies in politics and not having His support in our nation:

- 2008 - God raised up Mike Huckabee who fears God for president. Instead, Democrats voted for Obama and Republicans, in the primary, supported Mormon Mitt Romney and John McCain. Since this is a covenant breaking act, God sold the USA to Obama.

Healthcare has been greatly destroyed, the debt grew, abortion expanded, wars continued, and we saw widespread conflict between races and classes.

- 2012 - God raised up Christians, but conservatives and liberals forsook God by voting for Romney and Obama. God, in wrath, continued to sell the USA to Obama, who unwisely allowed gay sin in the military, raised the debt, gave ISIS weapons, continued wars, and aided illegal aliens with anti-American ways.

- 2016 - God raised up Mike Huckabee and others. Voters helping the ungodly (Clinton, Sanders, Trump...) caused more judgment. In 2015 there was the unconstitutional Supreme Court same-sex marriage opinion, men using women's bathrooms, Obama conceded to Iran, job losses to foreigners, Syria became dangerous, and Obama brought Muslim refugees in who have terrorism connections.

This further reveals that *family values* voting is not enough, since it supports those who believe in families but aren't required to be faithful Christians. We have seen that the fruit of *family values* only is God's judgment with our future at risk. Instead, the Biblical way is to only support Christian leaders who diligently follow God as Scripture teaches.

It is not because God is unaware of voters helping His enemies that the USA has not been completely destroyed. God has mercifully given us time to repent and turn to Him. Every Christian and church should fall on our faces and ask God for mercy for our sins. Churches staying out of politics put our nation and cities in danger.

We must make the commitment to only choose Christian leaders. If a Christian isn't running, then every church should have ongoing prayer and fasting for God to give us Christian leaders and so our consciences won't let us help the ungodly. Our duty to God is to vote for Christians, not just to vote.

Christian Laws Heal Our Land

In this modern world some may think that we can't have Biblical laws now. But we need to think this over. Would we really lose our freedom by following God? Eve only knew her relationship with God and Adam. She was deceived by a lie and then had to face judgment and lose many blessings.

At which point was she truly free? When she walked and talked with God? Or when she exercised her free will to do things her way? We don't realize it, but we are losing our freedom and civil liberties because of the judgment for disobeying God. So we need to ask ourselves if we are free following our will, or choosing to follow God's will?

Unreasonable people give excuses to resist God and not to honor His Holy Word like, "respect all beliefs," "tolerance," or "diversity," but we know that the Bible says, *God is angry with the wicked every day,* and we see that Christian bakers, florists, photographers, and others are losing jobs and bullied because of "diversity" (Psalm 7:11). Ever since the garden of Eden, Satan has been attacking God's Word. So it is the devil who tries to lead people astray not to build the USA on the Rock of God's Word.

To have God bless us, we must follow what Scripture teaches. We can't add to what God says and we can't subtract from it either. We are protected by following His Word!

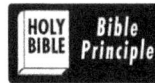

Christianity is part of the common law.

The good news is that God's Word filling our nation defeats Satan and evil. That is why I ask you to join me in praying often, *Father, we submit the USA to You in entirety. We want Your Word to fill our nation. In Jesus' name. Amen.*

To ensure that the USA was known for Christian character, our founders worked for all to know God's Word. This is one reason our government printed the Holy Bible and put it in schools so children would have piety and virtue.

Every law against the Bible is unjust. If we let our representatives defy God, then He judges us for this covenant breaking act. We know the First Amendment forbids Congress from making a law prohibiting the free exercise of Christianity. This means that laws against Christians are illegal according to the Constitution. Who will be bold enough to put the Ten Commandments back in courts? All of them have been in our laws since the colonialists arrived.

Why would God bless us for pagan laws? Abraham Lincoln said, *without [the Bible] we could not know right from wrong.*[9] To love God is to love His Word. To show our love for God, we can often pray, *Father, You are my and the USA's Lawgiver. I and the USA follow Your Word. In Jesus' name. Amen.*

The Bible Is the Rock on Which Our Republic Rests

To make the USA safe, we want the strongest foundation for our nation and God tells us that it isn't trusting in military ability, but that true security for our lives and family is by building our nation on Jesus Christ who is the Word of God (Psalm 11:3). The biggest threat to our national security is disobeying God.

HOLY BIBLE *Bible Principle*

No storm can harm the USA with the Bible as our foundation.

Jesus said, *Whoever... hears My sayings, and does them, I will show you to whom he is like: He is like a man which built a house, and dug deep, and laid the foundation on a rock: and when the flood arose, the stream beat vehemently upon that house, and could not shake it: for it was founded upon a rock. But he that hears, and does not, is like a man that without a foundation built a house upon the earth; against which the stream did beat vehemently, and immediately it fell; and the ruin... was great* (Luke 6:47-49).

Without looking at it, do you remember whose picture is on the $20 bill? It is Andrew Jackson, of course. He was a tough man, a general, and our seventh president, who said, "[The Holy Bible] is the rock on which our Republic rests."[9] Now when you see a $20 bill, remember what he said.

Daily Find God's Will with Scripture

Something you may not know about me is that I couldn't understand the Bible when I first read it in eighth grade. I struggled to comprehend what God was saying. But two years later when I learned that Jesus Christ is the only way to God—not anyone else—I was born again. God gave me the Holy Spirit. A light came on to make the Bible exciting. Now the best part of my day is to pray and learn God's Word.

The secret to learning the Bible is to have the Holy Spirit teach you. Before you read, pray, *Father, You are holy. I seek You with all my heart and all my soul. Help me understand Your Word by Your Holy Spirit. In Jesus' name. Amen.*

If you ever don't feel near to God, have confidence that if you keep seeking Him and reading your Bible it is only a matter of time until God's presence will be seen. That is one reason why Christians typically pray and read one or more chapters of the Bible in the morning and evening. Then to walk close with Him, we think about God and His Word. All the Bible is God's Word. If you haven't read the whole Bible, you can make that a goal. It will make you stronger.

HOLY BIBLE *Bible Principle*

Getting back to the Bible brings the USA's revival.

The USA has great hope of revival when we see how many people turned to God in the great revival with King Josiah. The King *made a covenant before the LORD, to walk after the LORD, and to keep His commandments... with all his heart, and with all his soul, to perform the words of the covenant which are written in this book. And he caused all that were present... to stand to it... according to the covenant of God, the God of their fathers.* (2 Chronicles 34:29-32).

As the church leads our nation, I ask you to join me in re-affirming covenant with these *7 Bible Truths.* Be encouraged because the USA's revival is by getting back to God's Word. Good things happen to us by following the Word of God.

Americans Love the Bible

There is a saying that I love. It is the USA is the land of the Bible. But we must work to continue as the land of God's Word and fill all fifty states with verses like, *Blessed is the*

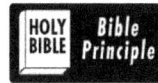

nation whose God is the LORD (Psalm 33:12) and *the LORD is our Lawgiver* (Isaiah 33:22).

The Bible is the book the Jamestown Settlers, Pilgrims, and Puritans brought with them. The Bible is the book that founded America and it is the book that saves the USA! Our duty is to teach all our nation that the inspiration, sufficiency, and supremacy of God's Word is what sets it far above every other book. The Bible is the infallible Word of God and our final authority for all matters of faith and practice.

We know that God's written Word is the only reliable rule of faith we have. There is nothing truthful that opposes the Bible. God's Word is the only standard that Americans have for doctrine and laws, for everything contradicting Scripture is a lie and false teaching.

Only the Bible heals our souls. There is no self-help book, seminar, or anything that will benefit our well being like His Word. The Bible puts our lives back together and leads us to Heaven. God speaks to us when we read His Word and the Bible is the only book that God requires us to read.

Following God's Word Will End Our Crisis

There is great hope for our nation to solve every problem by following Scripture. Everything we love as Americans returns when we do what is right before God. Can He and our covenant Christian nation rely on you? Have you made the decision that the LORD is your Lawgiver?

Protection, the healing of our lives, and fixing political problems are from following God's Word. To transform our lives from living in a nation under God's judgment to having a blessed USA, we follow God's Word.

The people and businesses who do what God says for our beloved country are national heroes, as they are the ones responsible for our freedoms, just laws, and healthy families. Those who refuse to follow God's Word are not on God's side, so to end judgment we turn away from them (2 Timothy 3:5).

As each of us desire to do God's will, if there is an area where you can better keep God's Word in your life, then agree to do it. In the following prayer make the decision to obey the Holy Bible with all of your heart and all of your soul.

Next, we will know the USA's true ruler more closely.

✝ *Prayer*

Father, Americans love Your Word. You are my and the USA's Lawgiver. We ask for the Holy Bible to fill our homes, government, schools, courts, and military. The Holy Bible is the Rock on which our Republic rests. Christianity is part of the common law. In Jesus' name, Amen.

✓ *Summary and Reflection Questions*

Jesus Christ is the Word of God and the Holy Bible is the book of the covenant. We know only the Bible is the Word of God. By deciding the LORD is our Lawgiver, we do His will.

To help save the USA, we need exceptional churches that teach God's Word for politics like the colonial churches did. This will restore respect to Christians. Some quick wins are for pastors to teach that we are to fear God not government and to only choose Christians who fear God for leaders.

Do you want God's protection? Then build your life and the USA on the Rock of God's Word. By following the Holy Bible, God blesses you and our country.

1. *What is Jesus Christ telling us in Luke 6:46-49?*
2. *Why does God bless us for having the Bible as the Rock on which our Republic rests? What are His blessings?*
3. *Explain the Bible's five requirements for leaders. How often does your church teach these leader requirements?*
4. *What are a few examples of what it is to live with the LORD as the USA's Lawgiver?*

6

Fourth Truth—Jesus Rules Our Nation

"The LORD is our King..." Isaiah 33:22 KJV

Tensions were high. Resistance to tyrants was publicly viewed as obedience to God and liberty for every American. England saw that the people of our nation were confident that Jesus wanted them to obey Him, not King George. The English appointed governor of Boston reported in 1774, *If you ask an American, who is his master? He will tell you he has none, nor any governor but Jesus Christ.*[1]

Patriotically, our founders sounded, *No king but King Jesus,* as an American Revolution motto. This famous battle cry affirms that Jesus Christ rules our nation and the USA lives for Him. This is why we are *One Nation Under God!* They recognized Jesus' authority and we need to follow their example and confess that Jesus is our King and authority.

Fourth Bible Truth
to end God's judgment
Isaiah 33:22, Phil. 2:11

Have no king but King Jesus

Why? Jesus brings the Kingdom of God's blessings of liberty, abundance, and peace.

Bible Blessings: How to Guarantee God Will Save the USA and Bless You

The Fourth Bible Truth is God will save the USA and bless you for having "no king but King Jesus". Jesus reigns as King in majesty and glory, whether we obey Him or not. Our judgment ends when we are in right relationship with Jesus Christ. Psalm 47:7-9 declares, *For God is the King of all the earth... God reigns over the heathen; God sits upon the throne of His holiness... the shields of the earth belong unto God.*

Each of us will give an account of our lives to Jesus on the Judgment Day so it is important to follow Him (2 Corinthians 5:10). We are stewards of what God has given us and we want to hear Christ say, "Well done" to our work (Matthew 25:21).

If you are a Christian, then you know Jesus Christ as your Savior. He gave Himself to save you, all He has including His life. Imagine the day and what you will do when He wraps His hands with the nail prints around you and says, "I love you" and welcomes you to Heaven. Jesus Christ is the only one who can save your soul. If you are not a Christian, today is the day to call on Him to save you from your sins. The moment you are born again, God delivers you from the devil's kingdom, the power of darkness, and translates you into the Kingdom of His dear Son. Jesus is your King (Col. 1:13).

Jesus is also the Son of Man who we identify with and He understands us. He lived a sinless life even though He was tempted in all things. As the Son of God, we worship Jesus Christ; He is God in the flesh.

When we realize how powerful and majestic He is and how much He cares for us by being crucified for us at Calvary, then we passionately declare I want to know Him more. His love for us increases our desire to be near Him.

83

Highly educated Paul, the apostle, counted all that he gained as loss compared to knowing Jesus. *That I may know Him,* said Paul, as he daily yearned to walk close with the Lord (Philippians 3:10). The reward of knowing Jesus more is infinitely greater than other things in life. We know Him by reading the Bible, the Spirit, and spending time with Him.

Jesus is unlike any other ruler because His Kingdom is grace and truth. He is the King of holiness. He wants you to be with Him because you have eternal life in Him. No other leader compares to our Lord who gave everything for you. The Kingdom of God is where liberty, abundance and peace exist, as well as righteousness, protection, joy, healing, and every good thing. Since Jesus is King of the Kingdom of God, serving Him is mandatory to solve our nation's problems.

Can you think of a good reason not to have Jesus Christ as the USA's King? Why would God bless our nation and deliver us from tyrants not listening to us if His Son is not our ruler?

From Adam to Samuel, God's people had no earthly king for they lived with God as their King directly. With the LORD as King, Noah was spared judgment, Israel defeated the greatest military power, and Joshua took Jericho. Our founders covenanted and made Jesus King of the USA and our republic has seen grace, miracles, and victories from God.

Jesus Christ is the Sovereign of the Universe

Since Jesus is the ruler of everything, we are to live exalting Him above every other person. God testifies, *That at the name of Jesus every knee should bow, of things in heaven, and things in earth, and things under the earth; And that every tongue should confess that Jesus Christ is Lord, to the glory of God the Father* (Philippians 2:10-11 KJV).

We honor Him as superior to all political leaders for He is the *KING OF KINGS, AND LORD OF LORDS* (Revelation 19:16; 1:5, 1 Tim. 6:15). He is subject to no one, other than the Father, and all things are subject to Him. All things are done according to His counsel and all authority in Heaven and earth has been given to Him (Colossians 1:16, Matthew 28:18).

Jesus sits at the right hand of God the Father. Higher than the angels, His throne is forever and ever; of His Kingdom there shall be no end (Hebrews 1:8, Luke 1:33). We know that His wrath is on the earthly leaders who don't follow Him (Psalm 2:2-5). Pharaoh found out the LORD is a man of war.

Jesus Christ was in the beginning with God; He is our Creator. All things were made by Him with the Father and Holy Spirit (John 1:1-3). We exalt Him because He is God and in Him all things exist (Hebrews 1:2-3, 6, Colossians 1:17). The earth and the heavens will perish, but He will always exist (2 Peter 3:10-11). He is the Alpha and the Omega, the Beginning and the End, the First and the Last (Revelation 22:13).

As the Judge of mankind, we have confidence that He will not acquit the wicked. He knows everything about everyone and He knows more about each person than even they know of themselves. He pardons the sins of all who come to Him.

Along with the Father and the Holy Spirit, Jesus Christ is Elohim (our Creator), Jehovah (my LORD God), Adonai (master and Lord), El Shaddai (God Almighty, my supply, my nourishment), Jehovah Jireh (my provider), Jehovah Rapha (my healer), Jehovah Nissi (my banner, victory), Jehovah Mikadesh (my sanctifier), Jehovah Tsidkenu (my righteousness), Jehovah Shalom (my peace), Jehovah Rohi (my shepherd), and Jehovah Shammah (the LORD is there). Jesus Christ is the great I AM.

Those who oppose Jesus are doomed because God is making Jesus' enemies His footstool (Hebrews 1:13). In judgment Jesus treads the winepress of the fierceness and wrath of Almighty God (Revelation 19:15). Everyone against Jesus Christ will be cast into the lake of fire and brimstone.

Yet Jesus is not willing that anyone should perish, so He sacrificed His life to bring you into His Kingdom. If you believe in Him, then you shall see His face and His name shall be on your forehead. You shall serve Him and reign with Him forever (Revelation 22:3-5). He delights in you!

With grace and mercy He helps you when you are in need. He is not a respecter of persons, so He helps all who call on Him—the poor and the rich, the sick and the healthy, and everyone who desires Him. He governs by serving us (Luke 22:26). At the name of Jesus, devils flee, the sick are healed, the bound are free, and the devil is powerless (Luke 10:19).

Our thoughts are to be on Jesus Christ because He is glorious. When I think about His dominion, kindness, love, majesty, and power, I worship Him! I declare, "Jesus, You are my King. I want to know You more; I surrender everything to You." Heaven proclaims He is worthy *to receive power, and riches, and wisdom, and strength, and honor, and glory, and blessing* (Revelation 5:12)! What is your response to Jesus?

Daily Live with Jesus as King

Our future is beautiful with Jesus as our King since "His Kingdom rules over all" (Psalm 103:19). Having no king but King Jesus isn't reserved only for when we get to Heaven. It is a daily, moment-by-moment walk with Him. To live with Jesus as your leader, first acknowledge Him as your King. Then during the day thank Him for His goodness and obey Him by faith, submitting to His authority (Matthew 16:24).

Why do we say, "Jesus Christ is Lord of the USA"? The answer is the USA has the Kingdom of God blessings through Him. We have liberty, prosperity, peace, brotherly love, and every good thing. To be free of dictators, Shariah law, and communism, then daily live with Jesus Christ as the leader of our nation. Where He rules, there are no evil rulers. That is why tyrants oppose Christianity, but Jesus is stronger than all evil persons and lovingly removes them to protect His people.

President George Washington reminds us to, "unite in most humbly offering our prayers and supplications to the great Lord and Ruler of Nations..."[3] Jesus gives us much to be thankful for. Unbelievers miss so much by not having God's

Kingdom. No forgiveness. No protection. No deliverance. However, with Jesus ruling us, we have all these blessings.

Romans 13: Is Jesus or Sinful Government King?

To save the USA from destruction, we have an important decision to make of who we serve, so we stop provoking God. Some think they are to "submit to government no matter what" and try to justify it using Romans 13. But is that the message of the Bible? Instead of blessings, the sins of politicians not obeying Jesus cause God's wrath to our nation.

God destroyed Israel and Judah for the people tolerating the sins of the evil kings. The fruit of submitting to bad government against God is destruction. God says the USA could be taken captive for Obama's sins and those sinning in Congress and the Supreme Court (1 Kings 13:34, 2 Kings 21:11-13). But liberty is the fruit of following God rather than sinful leaders. This is proven with God freeing our founders and Moses for following God instead of tyrants (2 Cor. 3:17).

Americans are for good government that serves God and we reject corrupt politicians, because that is how God is. He is sovereign. He is with those who are with Him (2 Chronicles 15:2, 2 Tim. 2:12). He says to leaders, "Kiss the Son, lest He be angry" and they "perish from the way, when His wrath is kindled" (Psalm 2:12). The reason the USA submits to Jesus Christ is the government is upon His shoulders (Isaiah 9:6).

We believe the Declaration of Independence is a rejection of ungodly rule. King George no longer rewarded good and punished evil as God commands (Romans 13:4, 1 Peter 2:14). So our founders fulfilled the responsibility of New Testament believers *to obey God rather than men* (Acts 5:29). This is the rule of Scripture. To love God is the First Commandment, so God is our ruler not anyone else. To love our neighbor as ourselves is the Second Commandment. But tyrants imposing their will on people, break these laws. That cannot be right.

The Hebrew midwives, Rahab, Daniel, Joseph and Mary, the wise men, Peter, Paul, John, and all the righteous obeyed God not sinful rulers. God says, *The midwives feared God, and did not as the king of Egypt commanded them... Therefore God dealt well with the midwives (Exodus 1:17, 20).* Since the Bible teaches that God blesses those who obey Him, refusing to follow unjust laws against Scripture, it is an erroneous belief to "submit to government no matter what".

Hope: Good Government Honors Christians

The misinterpretation of Romans 13 has caused the USA great troubles; it does not bring God's favor. Even with evil laws that bring God's wrath, some say, "obey them". But it is a sin to support oppression, or to reward evil and punish good. American history gives us the correct teaching.

HOLY BIBLE *Bible Principle*

With Jesus as your King, you see the Kingdom of God.

Among those who found Christian refuge in America are the Huguenots, where many of our courageous founders come from. They put God first. A Huguenot tract, "A Defense of Liberty against Tyrants," answers this question: Are we to have obedience to princes or God? All are to obey God for *all men... are His servants, farmers, officers and vassals, and owe account and acknowledgement to Him, according to that which He has committed to their dispensation; the higher their place is, the greater their account must be.[4]*

Liberty sermons like "A Discourse Concerning Unlimited Submission and Non-resistance to the Higher Powers" in 1750 by Jonathan Mayhew say it is good to submit to leaders serving God, but wrong to obey *tyrannical, oppressive rulers* as Romans 13 means leaders *are supposed to fulfill the pleasure of God... But how is this an argument for obedience to such rulers as do not perform the pleasure of God, by doing good; but the pleasure of the devil, by doing evil; and such as are not, therefore, God's ministers, but the devil's![5]*

Under God *We the People* are in charge. Elected officials are not above the Bible, us, or the Constitution (1 Peter 2:13). Reading Romans 13 in the King James Bible explains it better for it uses "higher powers" not "governing authorities". God is the highest power. Then the Constitution is the "supreme" law of the land. Looking at it this way matches the rest of the Bible.

Moses obeyed God as his King not Pharaoh. *By faith he forsook Egypt, not fearing the wrath of the king; for he endured, as seeing Him who is invisible* (Hebrews 11:27 KJV).

A mother is often the strongest earthly bond, but King Asa knew honoring God over his mother was God's will and would heal the land. So Asa *removed her from being queen, because she had made an idol in a grove: and Asa cut down her idol, and stamped it, and burnt it* (2 Chronicles 15:16 KJV).

Some say, "honor the king," but the USA isn't a man-made monarchy (1 Peter 2:17). Remember, we are a Christian Republic with a Constitution, so churches must correctly teach to: (1) Honor the Bible above all and (2) Honor the Constitution. Those who say to submit to congress, the president, or the courts when they violate the Constitution disobey God's Word and break the law. Take time and confess this sin to God to heal out land if you have done this.

As a note, 1 Peter 2:17 says, *Honor all men. Love the brotherhood. Fear God. Honor the king.* The word "honor" is used for all men and the king. We need more people saying to fear God. Jesus said, *fear not them which kill the body, but are not able to kill the soul: but rather fear Him which is able to destroy both soul and body in hell* (Matthew 10:28 KJV).

We honor politicians, courts, and police who serve God and follow the Constitution. But how can we honor those who violate the First Amendment and persecute Christians, or against our safety disregard the Second Amendment and try to disarm Americans, or violate the Fourth Amendment with warrantless searches, as these acts are against Americans?

The church's greatest civic duty is to endorse Christian political candidates. Churches have never been taxed to begin with, as the First Amendment forbids taxing churches. But politicians, by the Johnson Amendment in 1954, talked many churches to be non-profit 501(c)(3)'s with the catch they wouldn't endorse a candidate to keep their tax free status.

Ministers fell for the scheme to not follow the Constitution, the law of the land after God's Word. As a result of pastors being silent, Christians have been persecuted, corruption abounds, and the USA's survival is at risk. To save our nation, churches either must speak up politically as a non-profit or start a NOT non-profit ministry and speak up politically. Let's obey the Constitution and get rid of the Johnson Amendment.

While the Bible shows unbelievers as leaders, they are for God's purpose of judgment. Then God judges those heathen leaders too. Babylon destroyed Judah when they turned away from God. Then the Medes and Persians conquered Babylon.

If you want God's favor restored, teach and pray for churches to be freed from this false teaching to submit to government against God. Our founders knew that a leader not following Jesus is in rebellion to God. Nimrod wanted people to follow him instead of God (Genesis 10:8-10).

The more our nation submits to Jesus, the more liberty we have. As the Bible teaches, those who refuse Jesus as King cause our problems as they don't recognize God's authority.

King Jesus Will Save the USA

Be encouraged for God promises, *The LORD is our king; He will save us* (Isaiah 33:22 KJV). We have great hope because God rewards faith with answered prayer. We see time after time in the Bible that the righteous *through faith subdued kingdoms* (Hebrews 11:33). With faith in God, America's enemies are defeated. Jesus Christ is the USA's Deliverer.

Our founders needed deliverance from tyrants, so our "first national anthem" in 1770 says, *We fear them not, we trust in God. New England's God forever reigns.* This song, *Chester,* was boldly sung in churches, as soldiers marched, and in homes to show that Americans are for liberty and resist tyranny. It was written by famous hymnist William Billings.

Singing about our King and trusting in Him gives our nation deliverance. "My Country 'Tis of Thee" turns our hearts to exalt God. *Our fathers' God, to Thee, author of liberty... Protect us by Thy might, Great God, our King.*

Rejoice! Having *no king but King Jesus* always defeats America's enemies. Serving Him is why we stand up for life, liberty, and the pursuit of happiness. Everyone must understand that it is Jesus who makes the USA free! As true Americans we love Him! With Jesus as our leader we show God that He has our allegiance and He ends our judgment.

Our liberty-loving nation must have *no king but King Jesus* so we are on God's side and have His freedom. Will you affirm that Jesus is the USA's King? If so, then with love for God in your heart, often share with as many people as you can, *The LORD is our king; He will save us* (Isaiah 33:22).

Next, we discover an easy tool to share the good news and raise up the next generations as godly Americans.

✝ *Prayer*

Father, Jesus Christ is my King and King of the USA.
The USA obeys Him, not anyone else. In Jesus' name. Amen.

✓ *Summary and Reflection Questions*

We long to know Jesus, who is our King and the sovereign of the universe. He is worthy of our worship and submission for He purchased us with His own blood.

If you want the Kingdom of God and to be free from evil, then you must have "no king but King Jesus." By living with Jesus as King of the USA, God gives us liberty and the Kingdom of God blessings.

1. *What does "no king but King Jesus" mean to you? How do you live with Jesus Christ as your authority?*

2. *Why do those refusing to call Jesus King cause God's judgment on our nation?*

3. *Why did God greatly bless our founders and Moses for obeying Him rather than ungodly rule?*

4. *With more people calling on Jesus as King of the USA, what additional blessings would you have?*

7

Fifth Truth—Disciple Hearts to Be Like Jesus

"Teaching them to observe all things whatsoever I have commanded you..." Jesus in Matthew 28:20 KJV

God desires for our nation to have hearts like Jesus, so we glorify God and do good to man. Living like Jesus makes our citizens exceptional. Our forefathers faithfully advanced the Kingdom of God to help America grow in Christ, with piety and virtue. They conquered every problem by faith. Nothing could stop the Holy Spirit in them. As stewards, they discipled Americans as their priority. Now it is our turn to teach to observe all things Jesus commanded us. We will have great wisdom, souls will be saved, Christians will be strong, and injustice will end (Matthew 28:19-20).

Jesus gave us the Great Commission and He said that part of our vital work for Him is *that repentance and remission of sins should be preached in His name among all nations* (Luke 24:47). The *all nations* includes our beloved USA.

Fifth Bible Truth to end God's judgment *Matt. 28:19-20, Is. 59:21*	**Make disciples of the USA** *Why? To raise godly generations.*

Bible Blessings: How to Guarantee God Will Save the USA and Bless You

The Fifth Bible Truth is God will save the USA and bless your life when you make disciples of the USA. Why? Because keeping covenant and raising godly generations ends our country's judgment.

God and our founders count on us to have our nation glorify Him. We should often ask ourselves, "What can we do for God and country?" We can teach that the LORD is the God of our nation, pray publicly in Jesus' name, and help put the Holy Bible and Christian prayer back in every school. Following God makes the USA a better place and protects future Americans from judgment.

All power is given to Jesus Christ in Heaven and in earth. Remember, the church leads our Christian nation, not the heathen. Jesus Christ is the Head of the church and we are His body. He needs us to train people with the Gospel, speak up to have Christian laws, teach to live in sexual purity, save marriages, and help everyone know what their God-given rights are. Some people think, "God can make disciples without my help." But why did Jesus say, if you love Him, "feed My sheep"? (John 21:17)

Others don't want to offend people, but Jesus Christ spoke the truth in love so people would go to Heaven, not hell. As a result, some were offended by the Word of God, but those who followed His wise words were saved and healed. We can bring revival by teaching those we know God's Word.

The Great Commission is part of living in covenant with Jesus Christ. Let's arise quickly and make disciples of Americans. This is the next step to advance the Kingdom of our Lord Jesus Christ and to restore Heaven's blessings to us.

93

12 Ways to Make Disciples

To have hearts like Jesus, teach Americans the following:

1. **Serve the LORD only**—not strange gods or anything else. *Matthew 4:10, Exodus 20:3*
2. **Have no king but King Jesus:** God is sovereign; we obey God's government. *Isaiah 9:6 & 33:22, Philippians 2:11, Revelation 19:6, 2 Timothy 2:12*
3. **Insist to have Christian religious liberty:** Advance the Kingdom of our Lord Jesus. *Mark 12:30, Gal. 5:1*
4. **Man is created with dignity:** Americans demand our God-given unalienable rights—*including life, liberty, the pursuit of happiness, property, and conscience. Genesis 1:27, Acts 5:29, Declaration of Independence*
5. **Instruct children to know God:** Put the Holy Bible and Christian prayer back in schools. *Isaiah 59:21*
6. **The LORD is our Lawgiver:** God only blesses Christian laws based on the Bible. *Luke 6:47-49, Is. 33:22*
7. **Work to have a covenant Christian nation Government** immediately that:
   1) Are Christians who fear God Ex. 18:21, 2 Cor. 6:14-18
   2) Calls for Christian religious liberty Mark 12:30, Gal. 5:1
   3) Insists we have God-given rights Gen 1:27, Acts 5:29
   4) Is truthful Exodus 18:21
   5) Hates covetousness Exodus 18:21
8. **Support Christians** in politics, business, and organizations—not the heathen. *2 Chronicles 19:2*
9. **Our Christian nation is pro-life.** *Matthew 5:17*
10. **Serve God, not mammon (money).** *Matthew 6:24*
11. **The USA is for traditional marriage only**—One man and one woman; we believe in sexual purity with no adultery or fornication. *Jude 7, 1 Corinthians 6:9-11*
12. **Biblically pray for government.** Pray daily for the people of our nation and our government to live the five points of #7 above.

12 Decisions to Have a Heart Like Jesus

If we want our hearts to be like Jesus, then we need to make these decisions that our founders made to show we are on the LORD's side. With love in our hearts, we must disciple everyone we know to do the same by teaching the following.

Note: To show the context some quotes repeat from earlier. For further personal study and as a tool for ministries, writers, and students, see "The American Disciple Making Team Handbook".

Will you make these decisions:

Decision 1: I serve the LORD only and renounce all other gods. The USA is a Christian nation.

- Jesus said, "You shall worship the LORD your God, and Him only shall you serve" (Matthew 4:10).
- "Those nations only are blessed whose God is the Lord." Abraham Lincoln[1]
- "This is a Christian nation" Supreme Court[2]
- The blessings of serving the LORD mean that we are God's people with His blessings, abundance and protection (2 Corinthians 6:16, Psalm 33:12, Psalm 37:40); The judgments for false gods are provoking God to wrath and perishing (Deuteronomy 32:16-18, 8:19-20).

Decision 2: The LORD is my King. The USA has no king but King Jesus. We obey God's government.

- "The government shall be upon His shoulder" (Isaiah 9:6 KJV).
- "For the LORD is our judge, the LORD is our lawgiver, the LORD is our king; He will save us" (Isaiah 33:22 KJV).
- "That at the name of Jesus every knee should bow... every tongue should confess that Jesus Christ is Lord" (Phil. 2:10-11).
- Government, "Devoutly recognizing the Supreme Authority and just Government of Almighty God, in all the affairs of men and of nations..." Abraham Lincoln[1]
- The blessings of Jesus as our King are: God saves the USA, liberty, abundance, national security, and the Kingdom of God. The judgments for serving others are darkness, tyranny

and destruction (Isaiah 33:22, Colossians 1:13, John 8:12, 2 Corinthians 3:17, Matthew 6:33, 1 Kings 13:34, Luke 18:6).

Decision 3: Like our founders, I call for Christian religious liberty, not religious liberty of false gods.

- "You shall love the Lord your God with all your heart, and with all your soul, and with all your mind, and with all your strength" (Mark 12:30).
- "Stand fast therefore in the liberty with which Christ has made us free" (Galatians 5:1).
- Praying in Jesus' name and reading the Bible is Congress' first act. George Washington ordered the military to attend Christian church. The Bible was in schools from 1607-1962.
- The blessings for demanding Christian religious liberty are advancing the Kingdom of our Lord Jesus Christ and Christians are honored. The judgments for false gods are destruction (Matthew 28:19-20, Ezekiel 23).

Decision 4: I am created with dignity in the image of God. No one can take away my unalienable rights.

- "God created man in His own image" (Genesis 1:27 KJV).
- "We ought to obey God rather than men" (Acts 5:29 KJV).
- See the Declaration of Independence.
- The blessings for standing up for our God-given rights are Americans live free with our rights (2 Corinthians 3:17). The judgments for giving up rights is tyrants (Nehemiah 9:32-37).

Decision 5: Children are to know God. I will speak up for the Bible and Christian prayer to be in schools.

- "This is My covenant with them, says the LORD; My Spirit that is upon you, and My words which I have put in your mouth, shall not depart out of your mouth, nor out of the mouth of your seed, nor out of the mouth of your seed's seed, says the LORD, from this time and forever" (Isaiah 59:21).
- "Education is useless without the Bible." Noah Webster[3]
- George Washington told Indians, "I am glad you have brought three of the children of your principal chiefs to be educated with us... You do well to wish to learn... above all, the religion of Jesus Christ. These will make you a greater

and happier people than you are. Congress will do everything they can to assist you in this wise intention..."[4]

- The blessings for the Bible in schools are more children are saved and the USA has Christian character (Proverbs 22:6). The judgments for disobeying God are His wrath for breaking covenant and, sadly, more go to hell (Matthew 16:26).

Decision 6: The LORD is our Lawgiver. God is righteous, so I want laws based on the Holy Bible.

- "The LORD is our lawgiver" (Isaiah 33:22 KJV).
- "Whoever... hears My sayings, and does them... He is like a man which built a house, and dug deep, and laid the foundation on a rock: and when the flood arose, the stream beat vehemently upon that house, and could not shake it: for it was founded upon a rock" (Luke 6:47-48).
- "Christianity is part of the common law" Supreme Court[5]
- "[The Holy Bible] is the Rock on which our Republic rests," Andrew Jackson.[6]
- The blessings for making Christian laws are national security, health, and blessings. The judgments for disobeying God with non-Christian laws are curses, the USA being destroyed, and sickness (Deuteronomy 28, Luke 6:47-48, Exodus 15:26).

Decision 7: I will work and pray to have a Christian government immediately, as this is God's will.

- "Be ye not unequally yoked together with unbelievers: for what fellowship has righteousness with unrighteousness? and what communion has light with darkness? ... or what part has he that believes with an infidel?" (2 Corinthians 6:14-15).
- "Provide out of all the people able men, such as fear God, men of truth, hating covetousness; and place such over them, to be rulers" (Exodus 18:21).
- "When the children of Israel cried unto the LORD, the LORD raised up a deliverer to the children of Israel, who delivered them" (Judges 3:9 KJV).
- The blessings for a Christian government are the USA is exalted and blessed in all things (Proverbs 14:34, Psalm 1:1). The judgments for a non-Christian government are God's wrath and shame as a nation (2 Chronicles 19:2, Prov. 14:34).

Decision 8: I support Christians in politics, business, and organizations, not the heathen.

- "Should you help the ungodly, and love them that hate the LORD? therefore is wrath upon you from before the LORD" (2 Chronicles 19:2).
- The blessings of helping people, businesses, and ministries that follow God are He exalts our nation and rewards (Proverbs 14:34, Matthew 10:41). The judgments for helping the ungodly brings the wrath of the LORD and reproach (2 Chronicles 19:2, Proverbs 14:34).

Decision 9: God is pro-life so the USA is pro-life. I believe our country is to ban the sin of abortion again, honor father and mother, and repent of unjust wars.

- Jesus says, "You shall not kill" (Matthew 5:21).
- "They sacrificed their sons and their daughters unto devils, and shed innocent blood... Thus were they defiled with their own works.. Therefore was the wrath of the LORD kindled against His people, so that He abhorred His own inheritance. And He gave them into the hand of the heathen; and they that hated them ruled over them. Their enemies also oppressed them... they were brought into subjection" (Psalm 106:37-42).
- "Honor your father and mother" (Ephesians 6:2).
- "Love one another" (John 13:34 KJV).
- The blessings for being pro-life are a clear conscience, children, and happiness (Psalm 127:4-5). The judgments are God's wrath and tyrants as leaders, as is also the same judgment for unjust wars (Psalm 106:37-42). Honoring your father and mother results in long life (Deuteronomy 5:16).

Decision 10: I serve God, not mammon (money).

- "No man can serve two masters: for either he will hate the one, and love the other; or else he will hold to the one, and despise the other. Ye cannot serve God and mammon [riches]" (Matthew 6:24 KJV).
- The blessings for serving God are abundance (Matthew 6:33). The judgments for serving mammon (money) are God's wrath and many sorrows (1 Timothy 6:10).

Decision 11: God created male and female. To obey Him, the USA has traditional marriage only (one man and one woman for a lifetime). God calls for repentance of fornication, adultery, and homosexual sin.

- "Now the body is not for fornication, but for the Lord; and the Lord for the body" (1 Corinthians 6:13 KJV).

- "Be not deceived: neither fornicators... nor adulterers, nor effeminate [homosexuals], nor abusers of themselves with mankind [sodomites]... shall inherit the kingdom of God" (1 Corinthians 6:9-10 KJV).

- The blessings for God's Marriage of one man and one woman are strong families, God's favor, and more people go to Heaven. The judgments for disobeying God are He destroys gay nations in His wrath and unrepentant sinners don't go to Heaven (1 Corinthians 6:9-11, 2 Peter 2:6, Leviticus 18:25).

Decision 12: I will pray Biblically for the people of our nation and our government to fear God.

Why do we pray for our leaders? The Bible says the reason is "that we may lead a quiet and peaceable life in all godliness and honesty" (1 Timothy 2:2). To get this result, God's will is that we pray for our representatives to fear the LORD and to protect our God-given rights. This is more Biblical than praying for leaders to have wisdom since, "The fear of the LORD is the beginning of wisdom" (Proverbs 9:10). We must pray for all Americans to fear and love God, as under God *We the People* are in charge of our government.

While we do pray, "God bless America," we never pray for politicians disobeying God's Word that God would strengthen, protect, and bless them. We know He forbids that and judgment comes to those who help God's enemies (2 Chronicles 19:2, Romans 1:32, Psalm 129:5-8).

If politicians refuse to serve God, the Bible teaches for us to cry out to God for Christians who fear God to immediately replace those disobeying God. This is so we don't suffer in judgment by perpetuating their sin (Judges 3:9, 2 Corinthians 6:14-18, 2 Samuel 23:3).

Daily Biblical Prayer for Government™

Father,

The USA serves Jesus Christ. We devoutly recognize Your "Supreme Authority and just Government... in all the affairs of men and of nations". We love You and we love one another. May we and our representatives, schools, courts, law enforcement, and military:

1) Fear You, 2) Call for Christian religious liberty,
3) Insist to have our God-given rights of life, liberty, the pursuit of happiness, property, conscience...,
4) Be truthful, and 5) Hate covetousness.

We cry out for Christian leaders to immediately replace those in sin.

One Nation Under God. In God We Trust.

In Jesus' name. Amen.

Pray this daily prayer at home and with your church; it is based on: Isaiah 9:6, Mark 12:30-31, Exodus 18:21, 2 Cor. 6:14-18, Luke 22:26, Genesis 1:27, Judges 3:9. Include "by Rev. Steven Andrew" to reuse.

Wednesdays: Nationwide Prayer and Fasting

In addition to these *12 Decisions to Have a Heart Like Jesus,* you and your church are invited to participate in: (1) Nationwide prayer and fasting; (2) Christians Uniting to Save the USA™; and (3) The American Disciple Making Team™.

To heal our land, we pray and fast for our nation to repent of everything against Jesus Christ, since God only blesses us through His Son. The USA's hearts are to love God, so please join every Wednesday and ask your church to pray:

Father,

We exalt You, LORD, as the God of the USA. May Your will be done. We seek You to heal our land. To glorify You, and as our founders believed, the USA: serves You only, insists to have Christian religious liberty, wants the Holy Bible in schools, is pro-life,

100

and is for traditional marriage only. We desire to please You and we pray for everything against Jesus Christ to be removed from our nation in a peaceable way. We want a Christian government. As You say in Judges 3:9 and 2 Corinthians 6:14-18, we cry out for Christian leaders to immediately replace those disobeying You. Forgive our sins by Jesus' blood.

In Jesus' name. Amen.

2 Chronicles 7:14, Luke 11:2, Psalm 33:12, Matthew 4:10 & 5:21, Isaiah 59:21, 2 Peter 2:6, 1 John 3:8 & 1:7, Exodus 18:21, Judges 3:9, 2 Corinthians 6:14-18. Include "by Rev. Steven Andrew" to reuse.

Christians Uniting to Save the USA^{TM}

An amazing story is a conflict in the Continental Congress almost stopped our liberty from King George's oppression in 1774. Christians of different denominations weren't praying together due to denominational differences. However, to unite the USA in Christ and win the Revolutionary War, Samuel Adams arose and said, *I... can hear a prayer from a [Christian] gentleman of piety and virtue who was at the same time a friend to his country*[7] and the people agreed.

As Americans we must unite with every Christian of piety and virtue who loves the USA. If we have differences on doctrines, the seven things we must agree on are that we:

1. Insist to have Christian religious liberty and God-given rights
2. Keep covenant the USA is a Christian nation—*The LORD is the God of the USA and we are His people*
3. Call for Christian leaders in public service only, from school boards to president, not the heathen
4. Teach that *righteousness exalts a nation: but sin is a reproach to any people* Proverbs 14:34
5. Believe the Gospel of Jesus Christ
6. Have the LORD as our Lawgiver with the Holy Bible as our final authority
7. Obey the Constitution, which is after the Holy Bible is the law of the land and protects our God-given rights

See Chapters 3 and 5 for the information for these items.

101

Be Part of the American Disciple Making Team^{TM}

God wants every heart of the USA to love Him. That is why I want to ask you and your church to join the American Disciple Making Team^{TM} (ADMT). God calls all fifty states to unite in Christ as His all powerful American church.

Disciple making is to be part of our daily life. We make hearts to be like Jesus by sharing these 12 decisions and praying for our nation's hearts to love God more. Some ideas are to write articles or letters, make videos, blog, and start a home group to study this book. To make disciples, just share what you know of *God's Plan for the USA.*

How much time do you want to give to God? Can you give Him ten percent of your time? This is about two and half hours a day. Perhaps this could be: (1) An hour in the morning seeking and worshipping God; (2) An hour disciple making (meeting with someone, or sharing Bible verses by mail or online, or crying out to God for mercy for our country, or praying for our nation's hearts to love and fear God); and, (3) A half hour devotional time with God before you go to bed.

You will make a life-changing difference in people's lives by helping them grow as strong Christians. If you aren't ready for two and half hours, could you give God an hour a day? That could be twenty minutes of prayer and Bible reading morning and evening, and twenty minutes of discipling. If you have a family, be sure they get part of your discipling time.

This is the most important work. To be more effective, prayerfully schedule what you will do each day. For example:

Monday:	*5:00 - 6:00 pm*	*Disciple John*
Tuesday:	*5:00 - 6:00 pm*	*Share the 12 decisions online*
Wednesday:	*6:00 - 7:00 pm*	*Pray and fast for the USA*
Thursday:	*12:00 - 1:00 pm*	*Ask others to insist the USA has Christian religious liberty*
...		
Daily:	*6:00 - 7:00 am*	*Pray and read Bible*
	9:30 - 10:00 pm	*Pray and read Bible*

I pray for every person and church in the American Disciple Making Team™ daily, so let me know at my website that you joined. I will also provide you updates and share personal stories and tips. Helping to make disciples with these important decisions gives you a larger ministry.

There is great hope with the millions of faithful Christians in our nation. Just one covenant man, Moses, stopped God's judgment to Israel (Exodus 32). As Americans who love God, we have faith that the USA will be discipled and young Americans will live to glorify God! Your help will make a difference for God and in each person's life.

Next, we discover how to have times of refreshing.

✝ *Prayer*

Father, the USA serves You. Help us make disciples of our nation, from our homes and our churches to our government, schools, courts, and the military. In Jesus' name. Amen.

✓ *Summary and Reflection Questions*

Sharing the good news is God's will. These 12 Decisions to Have a Heart Like Jesus are our nation's and churches' priority to talk about. Can you help get the word out? By discipling hearts like Jesus we keep covenant, raise godly generations, end Christian persecution, and save the USA.

1. *How is the USA blessed by only serving the LORD?*
2. *What blessings does God give for having the Bible in schools? What are the judgments for disobedience?*
3. *Why is it urgent that we work and pray together to unite the USA in Christ as our founders did?*
4. *In what ways can you help teach these 12 ways to follow Jesus Christ? What can your church do?*

8
Sixth Truth—Victory Over Sin

"He took courage, and put away the abominable idols..."
2 Chronicles 15:8 KJV

History is filled with holy conflict when God's people rise up and publicly turn from their wicked ways and sinful relationships. Our consciences awaken us of acts and thoughts we do that grieve God and we have a deep conviction of sin. This decision to please God instead of man was made abundantly clear during the Great Awakenings in America with our nation having an intense desire to glorify God, as well as during the reigns of Asa and Josiah, when Judah turned from false gods and perversion.

With great courage King Asa and the people arose to stop the apathy about sin, so their troubles from God's judgment would end. The Bible shows that Judah killed the wicked people refusing to follow God as they used to do in Old Testament times before Jesus Christ came (2 Chronicles 15).

King Josiah also loved God and did the same, burning the idols of false gods and removing evil priests, leaders, and all things causing the suffering of the nation (2 Kings 23:4-24).

Likewise, in holy conflict Moses boldly called those on the LORD's side to kill the people refusing to repent, so God wouldn't destroy Israel when the people forsook Him by turning away from God to worship a gold calf (Exodus 32).

Today we remove evil differently; we *turn away* from those who refuse to repent (2 Timothy 3:5, Romans 16:7, 1 Cor. 5:13, James 4:7). God wants us free of evil so we simply *separate* ourselves from those against God. We read the Old Testament accounts of killing through the New Testament lens to identify and *turn away* from those in rebellion to God.

How to Have Times of Refreshing

To save our nation, the church, as the true leader of the USA, needs to unite and courageously repent of sins. *The Sixth Bible Truth is turning away from everything against Jesus Christ will save the USA and bless you. We do this to love God and to heal our land.* The early church repented upon hearing God's truth. They shook the dust off their feet to those who refused to obey the Gospel, as Jesus said (Luke 9:5); they removed sinful things like idols, perversion, and the occult from their houses. *Many of them also which used magic arts brought their books together, and burned them* (Acts 19:19).

Sixth Bible Truth to end God's judgment 2 Tim. 3:5, 2 Chron. 15:8	Turn away from everything against Jesus Christ
	Why? To love God and to heal our land.

Bible Blessings: How to Guarantee God Will Save the USA and Bless You

Opening the windows to breathe fresh air and taking the trash out to revive your kitchen is like repentance. But turning away from sin does more than that. It frees us from darkness!

Our safety is at stake from our national disobedience; sin puts our national security at risk. So that *times of refreshing may come from the presence of God,* we turn from sin and separate from those God calls *wicked* (Acts 3:19, Psalm 7:11).

I thank God for you who want to heal our nation. To have blessings we must overcome evils which our founders never allowed. Light and darkness cannot exist together. God says to: renounce other gods; turn away from His enemies; repent of tolerance of abortion, the occult, homosexual, and other sins; and remove the lie of separation of church and state.

Turning from False Gods Brings Blessings

God is holy. Other gods provoke Him to wrath, since forsaking Him is a covenant breaking act. The Bible forbids turning to false religions such as Muslims and Buddhists, as well as cults like the Jehovah's Witnesses and Mormons. Satan uses these false beliefs to lead people away from God.

Let's look at when Aaron the high priest and the Israelites made their own god, a molten calf of gold, to go before them instead of the LORD. The people saw Moses was delayed in returning with God's instructions. Some thought Moses died, but he was seeking God for Israel's future (Exodus 32).

By not trusting in God and seeking another deliverer, the people committed spiritual adultery to God. Aaron didn't stop the people from going astray with false gods, but misled them and fashioned a golden calf and said, *these be your gods, O Israel, which brought you up out of the land of Egypt* (Exodus 32:4). Then they celebrated their man-made god and caused shame with immorality and called this a feast unto the LORD.

They were breaking covenant, which provoked God. He said to Moses, *let Me alone, that My wrath may burn hot against them and I may consume them* (Exodus 32:10). But Moses asked God to turn from His fierce wrath. Then Moses confronted Aaron and burned the gold calf in fire and ground it to powder; he scattered it on the water and made the Israelites drink it. God and Moses responded this way because other gods are God's enemies leading into darkness.

Moses told them they "sinned a great sin" (Exodus 32:30). To spare the people and families that would repent from the judgment for this sin, Moses made everyone make a decision, asking, *Who is on the LORD's side? let him come unto me* (Exodus 32:25-26). God's response was to kill those who

106

wouldn't follow Him and plague the people for their god. This serious response is because they forsook God.

From this example, we learn how God views His people turning to the world for help. We see that Moses didn't sin but did what God said and killed about 3,000 rebellious men. Some say this is harsh, but forsaking God meant everyone would have been destroyed and not enter the promised land. Recall, today we don't kill those against God, but what we do is "turn away" from those who won't follow God.

For God to bless us, we must repent of false gods. To do this: (1) Share with everyone that strange gods bring judgment and the USA could perish (Deuteronomy 8:19-20); (2) Call for government and school prayer to be in Jesus' name; (3) Only vote for true Christians; and (4) Teach the Bible verses about serving the LORD only. My book, *The American Disciple Making Handbook,*[TM] provides these verses.

Looking at modern gold calves, we see several have fallen in sin, including ministers. With many involved, this could bring captivity or worse. Let's repent (Exodus 32, Ezekiel 23).

The USA Must Serve God Not Money

A false god that has crept in is serving money. In politics, business, and even in Christian circles, we find people serving money instead of God. Jesus said, *No man can serve two masters... Ye cannot serve God and mammon* (Matthew 6:24).

We often see liberals serving money and not God. For example, those who voted for Obama to get a freebie at other people's expense, such as Obamaphones or other public funds. We need to be wise since non-Christian politicians say things that may sound good, but voting for them can't please God.

Another example is supporting candidates with a worldly agenda such as those excelling in business or speaking instead of those who do God's will. Hillary Clinton and Donald Trump want men to use women's restrooms, prayed with Muslims and other false gods at the National Conventions, and believe clerks should give same-sex marriage licenses.[1]

Even though Trump admitted he never asked God's forgiveness, ministers prayed for Trump misleading Christians to a gold calf instead of to God. David Jeremiah prayed, Trump "will help us economically and spiritually and every way in this nation,"[2] but helping worldly people causes His judgment (2 Chronicles 19:2). Hopefully, these ministers will repent since this is a great sin to be ashamed of. We know God says, *Adulterers and adulteresses... friendship of the world is enmity with God... whosoever therefore will be a friend of the world is the enemy of God* (James 4:4 KJV).

Mormons Aren't Christians

Another great sin to confess to God is turning to Mormons in politics (Exodus 32:21). Paul warned us not to receive those who preach another Jesus or another spirit or another gospel (2 Corinthians 11:4). He also taught, *If any man preach any other gospel unto you than that ye have received, let him be accursed* (Galatians 1:9 KJV). Should you vote for someone like that? If God says they are accursed, why would you want them in the White House or on a school board?

One of the most common misconceptions that needs to be exposed to have God's healing is that Mormon's are perceived as Christians and "good people". But the Bible teaches Mormons are deceived and serve a false god (Matthew 4:10). Many people naively consider them to be Christians, but they are historically classified as a cult and forbidden by God for leadership since they turn our nation away from the LORD.

Jesus Christ is God eternal and God's Son, but Mormons negate this and teach that Jesus is the spirit brother of Lucifer. The devil has never been on the same level as Jesus Christ. These lies are satanic in nature. What would you do if someone said your child is the spirit brother of Lucifer? You would tell them to never come back. Due to their false teaching, Mormons were often chased out of town. The Mormon false god cannot save your soul or help the USA.

	Christianity - *Truth*	**Mormon Cult -** *Error*
God	Always God eternally *Deut 33:27; Is. 43:10*	An exalted man; Mormons think God was first a man
Jesus Christ	Is God; Creator along with the Father and the Holy Spirit *Gen 1; John 1:1-3*	A created being, the spirit brother of Lucifer; Mormons have "another Jesus" *2 Cor. 11:4*
Holy Spirit	Is God; Comforter, Teacher, and Given to Christians *John 14:26*	Mormons have a "different spirit" not the Holy Spirit *2 Cor 11:4*
Holy Bible	God's Word, Final authority, Inerrant *2 Timothy 3:16-17*	Mormons have "another gospel" by adding to Scripture *2 Cor 11:4*
Salvation	Saved by grace through faith *Ephesians 2:8-9, John 3:16*	Saved by works and Mormonism
Man	Christians are children of God through faith in Jesus *John 1:12*	Exalted to become God and Godesses

The above shows the Mormon error. Mormons also admit their founder had up to 40 wives, even a 14 year old girl.[3]

We need blessings, but the Bible teaches turning to God's enemies for leaders threatens our survival. God says, *They have set up kings, but not by Me: they have made princes, and I knew it not... that they may be cut off* (Hosea 8:4 KJV).

Mormons Glenn Beck and Mitt Romney do not have God's answers for our nation. They have failed to end our judgment, since turning to those with strange gods, such as Mormons, provokes God and increases judgment (Ezekiel 23).

Some may think it doesn't matter who they voted for in 2012, but this sin must be confessed, along with those supporting Clinton, Sanders, Trump, and other ungodly people in 2016, to end our crisis. Otherwise, why should God stop judgment for this sin committed by millions of people? Working to remove tyranny without pleasing God has failed, as the real issue is how can the USA obey God so He removes the judgment of politicians who hate Americans.

Be encouraged for He wants to remove corrupt politicians, but since they are His judgment for false gods and other sins, turning to Romney and Beck backfired and made Obama stronger. After 2012, Republicans agreed to more debt, ISIS became a security danger, and Republican politicians funded Obamatrade, Obamacare, and illegal aliens.[4] The good news is following the *7 Bible Truths* removes this corruption.

I say this not to condemn anyone, for daily I pray for every American. Again, God sees no difference with Israel worshipping a gold calf and calling it Jehovah and those who turn to Obama or Mormons for leadership. He says, *Be ye not unequally yoked together with unbelievers: for... what communion hath light with darkness?* (2 Corinthians 6:14 KJV).

The Word of God Is Above Ministers

How did our beloved USA go from seeing Mormons as sinful to turning to them for help? The reason is ministers misled us. At one point I was considering, should I mention which ministers misled our nation? After praying, I knew God wanted me to correct this church problem to heal our land and as I wrote this, Romney went from leading the GOP in 2015 to dropping out. God has seen everyone grieved by this sin.

We must repent of turning to unbelievers, for it has caused our problems. *The LORD plagued the people, because they made the calf, which Aaron made* (Exodus 32:35 KJV).

Wanting the USA to obey God, I called our nation to select Christian leaders in the 2012 election. Sadly, many ministries did the opposite, angering God and misleading dear Christians to disobey the Bible to support Romney and/or Beck who endorsed Romney. I have privately contacted these ministers mentioned or their staff, if the person wouldn't talk to me, asking them to obey God. Let's hope all will repent because disobeying God's Word is a great sin.

Billy Graham hosted Romney and said, "I'll do all I can to help you."[5] But God says, *If... any... bring not this doctrine, receive him not into your house, neither bid him God speed:*

For he that bid him God speed is partaker of his evil deeds (2 John 10-11). This made evangelicals look weak in the media.[5]

The Billy Graham Evangelistic Association also removed listing Mormons from their website as a cult and misled the

HOLY BIBLE *Bible Principle*

Repenting of false gods heals our lives and saves the USA.

church with an article, "Can an Evangelical Christian Vote for a Mormon?"[5] The article told Christians, "The answer is yes" and that "God's principles" of voting for Romney cause "His blessing upon our nation"[5] even though God says to choose Christians and that turning to Romney provokes God to wrath (2 Chron. 19:2).

When asked if a Christian can vote for a Mormon, Franklin Graham said, "Yes, the fact that Mitt Romney is a Mormon doesn't bother me."[5] This is not a Christian statement. Both Graham's voting advice blocked the USA from having a Christian government that God blesses.

Joel Osteen said, "I see them [Mormons] as brothers in Christ" and when asked if it would be appropriate for Romney to speak at the largest Christian university (Liberty), Osteen replied, "It would be appropriate".[5] When questioned if a Mormon is a true Christian, Osteen answered, "In my mind they are."[5] This is the opposite of what the Bible teaches.

James Dobson has misled Christians with Romney since at least 2007 and shared, "I spent an hour and a half with him [Romney]. I liked him... he's still on the list".[5] Jerry Falwell Jr. had Romney and Beck speak to the Liberty student body.[5] Pat Roberston called Romney an "outstanding Christian".[5]

David Barton, John Hagee, TBN, Tony Perkins (Family Research Council), American Family Association (AFA), Kirk Cameron, Ray Comfort, Lou Engle, Rick Scarborough, Kenneth Copeland, Richard Land, Robert Jeffress, and others[5] either supported, or helped, Beck or Romney against Scripture.[5] Not one repented when I contacted their ministry.[6]

When asked if Obama was a Christian, Franklin Graham and Joel Osteen misled people to think Obama was a Christian even with Obama's support of Islam, abortion, homosexuality, and lying. Osteen said, "I just believe in all my heart that [Obama] is a Christian."[5] Graham answered, Obama "has said that he is a Christian. Leave it at that."[5] But Jesus teaches that we "shall know them by their fruits" (Matthew 7:16 KJV). Also 1 John 2:4 states, "He who says, I know Him, and keeps not His commandments, is a liar, and the truth is not in him."

To Heal Our Land, We Need Stronger Christian Leaders

Remember that God calls those, who give an okay to vote for or associate with a Mormon, Obama, Clinton, or Trump, "adulterers" (James 4:4) and He says they "played the harlot". Israel *played the harlot when she was Mine* (Ezekiel 23:5).

If we don't repent of helping God's enemies how can God protect us from our enemies? *Because they have transgressed my covenant... the enemy shall pursue him* (Hosea 8:1-3 KJV).

Adultery to God is most dangerous. It gives God the right to destroy the USA, so we must ask for mercy. He sees voting for unbelievers as despising His Word and the Bible says this causes more terrorism (Leviticus 26:15-16). To have God's favor, we must find ministers, like the colonial pastors, who faithfully teach the Gospel to only have Christian leaders.

Even ministers who evangelize, fight for pro-life, call for liberty, give Christmas gifts to children, pray and fast, teach on miracles, and oppose Islam commit adultery if they support Mormons or worldly people. Each of us must decide if we are on the LORD's side or not. God asks for our loyalty.

Honestly, I felt let down by these ministers and you may feel that they betrayed your trust, but God says to trust in Him not people. To be saved and walk with God all you have to do is follow Jesus Christ and the Bible. By trusting in Jesus for salvation and studying God's Word daily, you will keep your soul safe. I encourage you to pray, *Father, my loyalty is to You and to Your Word, the Holy Bible. In Jesus' name. Amen.*

Many voters wonder why God did not remove Obama. But God waits for them to be honest about the sin of not crying out for Christian leaders. God says, *None shall rescue him. I will go and return to My place, till they acknowledge their offense, and seek My face* (Hosea 5:14-15).

What prevented God from destroying our nation for Democrats and Republicans turning to God's enemies? The answer I find in Scripture is those who wanted a Christian government and obeyed God by refusing to sin by voting for unbelievers Obama and Romney, just as when Moses saved Israel by not compromising with the gold calf (Exodus 32).

The LORD is a jealous God. Not repenting of adultery is serious. In the Old Testament those who led people away from the LORD and to other gods were killed to stop God's wrath (Exodus 32:27, Deuteronomy 13, Leviticus 25). Israel's enemies defeated Israel until Joshua removed the accursed people when Israel transgressed covenant by taking an accursed thing (Joshua 7:1-12). Today, as the New Testament teaches, we just turn away from false teachers and those not repenting (James 4:4, 2 Timothy 3:5).

All strange gods are forbidden. The lie of universalism, which is when people think that everyone goes to Heaven, is sin too. The only way to go to Heaven is to believe in Jesus Christ to save you. But some ministers imply that Muslims and/or Mormons and/or atheists go to Heaven. This is false teaching. Jesus says, *I am the way, the truth, and the life. No one comes to the Father except through Me* (John 14:6 KJV).

Divide Politics as Christian and Heathen Rather Than Right and Left

We must repent of another sin. The devil is scheming to remove Christianity from politics by getting people to say they are "left" or "right" instead of Christian or non-Christian.

113

When we examine it, being a "liberal" or a "conservative" are unAmerican. By choosing a side we turn away from Jesus and choose how we want to sin. Therefore, we must repent of the "conservative" and "liberal" idols. God sees people as either Christian or heathen, not "conservative" or "liberal".

"Liberals" vote for "liberals" such as Obama, Clinton, or others who defy God with false gods, abortion, and gay sin. "Conservatives" vote for those on the "right' such as Trump, Romney, or other "conservatives" who don't fear God.

According to election analysis, 99.8% of voters disobeyed Scripture in 2012.[7] About 129 million voters betrayed Jesus Christ by choosing non-Christians Obama and Romney for leaders. Only around 200,000 put our Lord first by voting for Christians. The ungodly can't help us as only Christian leaders have the Holy Spirit, God's wisdom, Christian love, and favor.

How can Christian persecution end unless pastors teach that only Christian leaders are of God? Let's join Josiah who *did that which was right in the sight of the LORD... and turned not aside to the right hand or to the left* (2 Kings 22:2).

American Vs. Left/Right Extremists

AMERICAN †≡≡
Like founding fathers

Loves God and chooses Christians who fear God for leaders
(i.e. Mike Huckabee, Judge Roy Moore...)
- Keeps covenant that the USA is a Christian nation "to all generations"
- Demands Christian religious liberty
- Insists we have God-given rights
- No false gods; is pro-life and for traditional marriage only
- Lives to advance the Kingdom of our Lord Jesus Christ
- Follows the Constitution

On the LORD's side
Exodus 18:21, 2 Corinthians 6:14-18
- Cause God's blessings

LEFT
Liberal

- Votes for non-Christian leaders (i.e. socialists or communists Obama, Clinton, Sanders...)
- Defends Satan-given rights (abortion and gay sin)
- Denies the USA is a Christian nation
- Violates the Constitution

Enemy of God *James 4:4*
- Responsible for God's judgment
- UnAmerican and Extremist

RIGHT
Conservative

- Votes for non-Christian leaders (i.e. business people such as Trump, Mormon Romney...)
- Lukewarm about God-given rights including liberty
- Not 100% for pro-life and traditional marriage
- Violates the Constitution

Enemy of God *James 4:4*
- Responsible for God's judgment
- UnAmerican and Extremist

Neither the "left" or "right" represent the USA. These charts and the *American Christian Voting Guide*[TM] on my website[1] show God's will for politics and how far from our founders the "left" and "right" are. To fix our nation, vote only for true Americans since "liberals" and "conservatives" result in God's judgment and divide us. Some try to justify voting "left" or "right" as the lesser of two evils, but turning to unbelievers is a sin. It is like saying, "I voted for Baal not Molech," or a child saying, "Dad, I stole $9 instead of $10."

American Center Political Chart
Where does your politician fit?

SECULAR
"LIBERTARIAN"
Motive: Self
Duty: Serve Self
Rights: Man Made
Gov.: Leads to Anarchy
God: Ignores God
Wars: Defensive but Godless
Economy: Free Market Attempt

TEA PARTY

AMERICAN †
Like founding fathers
Motive: Advance the Kingdom of our Lord Jesus Christ & Enjoy the Liberties of the Gospel
Duty: Serve God
Rights: God-given: Life, Liberty, Pursuit of Happiness, Property, Conscience
Gov.: Christian Republic
God: The LORD
War: Defensive, Just Cause
Economy: God Blessed Abundance

On the LORD's Side
God's blesses

LEFT (Liberal)
Motive: Oppose Conservatives
Duty: Serve Government
Rights: Government-given
Gov.: Socialist
God: Anti-Christian
Wars: Aggressive
Economy: Debt-based

RIGHT (Conservative)
Motive: Oppose Liberals
Duty: Serve Big Business
Rights: Big Business-given
Gov.: Democracy
God: Any god (i.e. Mormon cult)
Wars: Aggressive
Economy: Debt-based

PROGRESSIVE

COMMUNIST
Motive: Fear
Duty: Serve Dictator
Rights: None (Police State)
Gov.: Dictator
God: Attack God
Wars: Unjust
Economy: Communist Slave

Shaded areas are responsible for God's Judgment
"Enemy of God" James 4:4
UnAmerican and Extremist

Moderate combines *Left* and *Right*

The devil uses "left" and "right" to infiltrate pro-life, traditional marriage, and liberty groups too. Christians give millions of dollars to organizations endorsing God's enemies, whether it is pro-life, marriage, family, or other groups. But God wants us to support those who only promote Christians.

Which battle will you fight? Will you: (1) Support true Christian leaders who advance the Kingdom of our Lord Jesus Christ and call for our God-given rights, or (2) Be a traitor to God with "liberals" (who mock Christians and promote same-sex sin) and "conservatives" (who don't serve the LORD only)?

The motive of the left is typically to oppose the right and vice versa. To get out of our problems, we need leaders like our founding fathers so God blesses us. The "left" and "right" are the real extremists who oppose America.

The USA Honors Life and Is for Traditional Marriage

God is pro-life and for the marriage of one man and one woman for a lifetime. He promises to heal our land by our nation repenting from shedding innocent blood and sexual immorality. In its most base form, abortion is simply murder. Sexual sins include fornication, adultery, and homosexuality.

When politicians promote sacrificing our children by spending about $1.5 billion in three years to abortion related companies, they break covenant and use our money against our consciences.[8] Our Christian duty is to end government funded abortion and to bring back the ban on abortions. This will stop more innocent blood crying out to God, for shedding innocent blood results in leaders who hate Americans as judgment; this sin is a curse that is causing so many of the problems in the USA (Psalm 106:37-42).

| HOLY BIBLE | Bible Principle |

The USA heals by repenting of abortion, fornication, adultery, and homosexual sin.

Here is God's hope. If you had an abortion or if you have guilt from another sin, ask God to cleanse your conscience with Jesus Christ's blood. God will remove the guilt (Hebrews 9:14). Jesus' blood will make your life whole.

Having the fear of God instead of tolerance of sin is God's agenda. God is intolerant of sin. That is why George Washington ordered the military, *To the distinguished character of a Patriot it should be our highest glory to add the more distinguished character of a Christian.*[9] About sexual purity, Jesus says to be married as one man and one woman, or to be single and celibate (Matthew 19:4-12).

In his popular dictionary, Noah Webster defined sodomy using Romans 1 as "A crime against nature." For God to bless the USA, Washington, the most respected American, court martialed sodomites and had, "Abhorrence and Detestation of such Infamous Crimes."[10] Recall, he also taught, "We cannot hope for the blessing of heaven on our army if we insult it by our impiety and folly."[11]

Our national security is very important. God says we are to trust in Him for our protection. That is why *In God We Trust* works. He also says, *When the army goes forth against your enemies, then keep yourself from every wicked thing (Deuteronomy 23:9).* With gay and other sins in the military, God doesn't go with them. Sin means the military loses wars. How can God be with a military against Him? Sin is very dangerous to the USA, so let God know that you are on His side and oppose everything against Him too.

Tolerance of homosexual sin means: (1) God's wrath as He promises to destroy gay societies. *Sodom and Gomorrah... going after strange flesh, are set forth for an example, suffering the vengeance of eternal fire* (Jude 7 and 2 Peter 2:6, Leviticus 18:25); (2) More people go to hell; (3) More Christians fired for obeying their conscience; (4) Safety dangers from men entering women's bathrooms; and (5) Health problems. The CDC reports that two in five gays have HIV and get 57% of the new HIV cases,[12] and studies show the average age of death for gays is between 39 - 43 years old.[13]

Those against God call our founders "haters" and "extremists" because they obeyed God's marriage. However, God calls our founders lovers of God. The real evil is being a hater of God and losing one's soul in hell. The Bible teaches that if the shamefulness of gay sin doesn't bother a person it is a sign of a reprobate mind, unapproved by God (Romans 1:28). There is no sign that they are going to Heaven.

What is the most Christ-like and compassionate response to gays and other sinners? Jesus Christ shows us. He said, *Repent, and believe in the Gospel* (Mark 1:15). He loves people and invites each of us to go to Heaven instead of hell.

To please God, we must stop watching immorality on TV, turn away from politicians tolerant of sin, and boycott companies promoting sin. If you have been tolerant of abortion or sexual sin, confess this to God (2 Chronicles 19:2).

Holy Civil Disobedience

It is shameful that the Supreme Court and Obama mock God, our founding fathers, and the USA with same-sex marriage. We know the Bible says they are God's enemies in rebellion and unashamed of sin. They scheme to change His ordinance of marriage (James 4:4, Romans 1:24-32, Isaiah 24:5). They declared war against God by opposing Christian religious liberty and our God-given right to obey conscience (Matthew 4:10, Mark 12:30-31).

The truth is they don't care if Christians lose jobs, are persecuted, or sin against our conscience. To stop God from destroying our country, we must speak up for Christian leaders to replace those against God.

Since God is our Lawgiver and Supreme Judge, we must follow Him. Same-sex marriage is defying God who created male and female. If we want to go to Heaven, not hell, we must obey God who says gay marriage is "wicked" (Genesis 13:13). While we are saved by grace, we must obey God. Those in rebellion to God, such as Sodom and Gomorrah who defied God are in hell. They didn't want to repent. Without holiness no one will see the LORD (Hebrews 12:4).

Boldly, Mike Huckabee defined it as "judicial tyranny" to jail Kim Davis because a high school civics class knows the Supreme Court can't make a law. Remember, laws are made by congress and executed by the president.[14]

Our founders call the whole nation to follow God not man. Exercising our God-given right to freedom of speech is guaranteed by the Bible and the Bill of Rights. All laws against Christians are illegal. The justices and Obama are violating the Constitution.

The First Amendment says, *Congress shall make no law... prohibiting the free exercise [of Christianity].* To obey God our founders, who wrote the Constitution, made homosexual sin illegal in all 13 colonies, as did all 50 states. The Supreme Court is lawless to God, our founders, and the Constitution.

God shows us how to respond to same-sex marriage. We and our churches are to: (1) Cry out to Him to deliver us from the tyranny (Judges 3:9, 2 Corinthians 6:14-18); (2) Speak up boldly that the USA obeys God rather than men; and (3) Teach that it is unconstitutional for the Supreme Court to make a law. These actions are required to establish law and order, as well as for civil disobedience to be effective.

As our nation's top priority, we must fight for Christian liberty in the USA. The reasons to obey the LORD are:

1. To love God - Our duty is to obey God's will of one man and one woman marriage (Matthew 19:4-6).
2. To go to Heaven - Lot was vexed by the sin of the sodomites and God saved Lot. But Lot's wife didn't fear God and lost her soul to hell where the worm shall not die and the fire is not quenched (2 Peter 2:6-9).
3. To save the USA - God is to be feared. He promises that same-sex marriage means certain destruction of the USA (Jude 7, 2 Peter 2:6, Leviticus 18:25).

To protect our future, every pastor and Christian must insist that Christians replace those against the LORD. God is not with them as they are not with God. Their sin curses them and we don't want to share in their judgment. Article III, Section 1 of the Constitution says, *the judges, both of the supreme and inferior courts, shall hold their offices during good behavior...* Theses justices and Obama are unrepentant. They knowingly targeted Christians for persecution, misled people to lose their souls by sin, and are unqualified to be leaders. The USA has no confidence in them (2 Chron. 19:2).

Will pastors be faithful to God and country by preaching to repent of gay sin, so Americans won't be jailed or fined for following God? If your minister won't publicly call for Christians to immediately replace these justices and Obama, then shouldn't you find a pastor who fears God and stands up for Him? As it was in 1776, it is today. Courageous pastors and Christians who insist that our nation serves Jesus Christ are the ones who will save the USA from destruction.

Renouncing the Occult Brings Healing

Another sin to repent of is the occult. Many Christians are unaware of the dangers of Satan's darkness, but the devil uses movies, books, schools, social media, and other sources to influence people with familiar spirits, psychics, talking to the dead, sorcery, numerology, fortune telling, horoscopes, meditation with demons, and witches. These deceptive sins bring judgment and open the door for bad things to happen to those involved (Deuteronomy 18:9-14).

A former witch I met said that she became a Christian since God had more power than the devil. Let's do all we can to protect every child from the devil. To help save their souls, we can buy children's Bible movies and use Vacation Bible School supplies at home. We must not allow children to watch demonic cartoons or read about evil spiritual powers.

There shall not be found among you anyone that... uses divination, or an observer of times, or an enchanter, or a witch, or a charmer, or a consulter with familiar spirits, or a wizard, or a necromancer. For all that do these things are an abomination unto the LORD (Deuteronomy 18:10-12).

We Repent of Separation of Church and State

To have God's favor, one more sin that we are to repent of is the lie of separation of church and state. It is unAmerican and provokes God because the USA's duty is to serve Him. Pastors and Christians must declare that our country follows the LORD and work for a government like our founders. My book, *Government Serves God,* shows separation of church and state is: (1) Not what our founders practiced or intended; (2) Not Constitutional; (3) Not historical; and (4) Sin.

The USA Chooses Victory Over Sin

God is light and sin is darkness. Light and darkness cannot exist together, as the homosexuals persecuting the Christian bakers, florists, and clerks shows. Either the USA follows Jesus Christ with sin subdued like our founders established, or people give themselves to sin with Christians persecuted and the nation in God's wrath. So let us flee from gold calves, Sodom and Gomorrah, and all sin. The good news is that times of refreshing come by repenting of everything against Jesus Christ.

Next, we will learn the hope of God's total forgiveness.

✝ *Prayer*

Father, I and the USA are on Your side. We repent of everything against Jesus Christ, including tolerance of other gods, turning to the heathen, abortion, homosexuality, the occult, and the lie of separation of church and state.
In Jesus' name. Amen.

✓ Summary and Reflection Questions

Sin puts our national security at risk. Part of covenant is to quickly turn away from what God opposes. This brings you and our nation His blessings and restoration.

1. To heal the USA, what sins must be repented of?

2. What childhood memories do you have of your family teaching to turn from sin?

3. Read 2 Timothy 3:5, 1 Corinthians 5:13, and Romans 16:7. Why do we turn away from the unrepentant?

4. What will you and your church do to help others repent and have victory over sin?

9

Seventh Truth—God's Mercy and Forgiveness

"You are a gracious God, and merciful,
slow to anger, and of great kindness." Jonah 4:2 KJV

It is not too late for the USA to receive God's mercy and forgiveness to end God's judgment and to heal our land. Why does God want to show mercy to the USA? He knows we need mercy for our great sins so our nation is not destroyed. False gods, same-sex marriage, and selling innocent aborted babies' body parts grieve the Holy Spirit. But God's mercy is greater than our sins. This is why we must confess our sins to God and be forgiven, which gives us hope.

There was a woman who had heard about Jesus and how the Lord changed so many lives. She had gone to see Him and heard Him speak about forgiveness. Her conscience reminded her of her guilt when she thought of all the things she had done. She knew she was a sinner and believed there was no hope of forgiveness for her.

Later, she heard that Jesus Christ was having dinner at a Pharisee's house. She was drawn to the Lord and stood behind Him weeping in desperation She humbled herself and fell at Jesus' feet, washing His feet with her tears, wiping them with her hair, and anointing them with oil. When the Pharisee saw this, he spoke to himself that Jesus shouldn't allow her to touch Him because of how sinful she was. But Jesus answered that those who have been forgiven more will love more. With compassion, He forgave her as she wept (Luke 7:36-50).

Jesus Christ desires to forgive. He forgave Peter for denying Him three times in His greatest need. The guilty find grace and mercy with the one Mediator between God and man. To the woman caught in adultery Jesus Christ said, *Neither do I condemn you. Go and sin no more* (John 8:11).

King David was to be put to death for committing adultery with Bathsheba and arranging for her innocent husband's death, according to the law. He was guilty and knew he deserved to die twice for his sins, so what did he do? He sought the covenant mercy of God. *Have mercy upon me, O God... Create in me a clean heart* (Psalm 51:1 & 10 KJV).

No one deserves forgiveness. We cannot earn it, or buy it. Our own merits or good works cannot forgive our sins. Yet, by putting our faith in Jesus for forgiveness we are forgiven.

God didn't destroy Nineveh when the people repented. *God saw their works, that they turned from their evil way; and God repented of the evil, that He had said that He would do unto them; and He did it not* (Jonah 3:10 KJV).

Our founders relied on God's forgiveness for our Christian nation's sins with days of prayer and fasting. Abraham Lincoln proclaimed that our country can be forgiven, *It is the duty of nations as well as of men... to confess their sins and transgressions, in humble sorrow, yet with assured hope that genuine repentance will lead to mercy and pardon...*[1]

God's great mercy has prevented our country's destruction. Jesus pleads for the USA to be spared even though public schools oppose Him and some churches have taken down their crosses. He sees there are faithful Americans who apply Jesus Christ's blood to our nation. The good news is that our covenant with God means there is forgiveness. To experience God's grace, we turn to Jesus Christ. The closer we are to Him, the more grace we know.

God is Satisfied with the Sacrifice of Jesus

As the Lamb of God, Jesus lovingly laid down His life for us to redeem us from our sins, the innocent for the guilty. "For He has made Him to be sin for us, who knew no sin; that we might be made the righteousness of God in Him" (2 Corinthians 5:21).

Seventh Bible Truth to end God's judgment *1 John 1:7, Jonah 4:2*	**Restore the Cross and pray to receive forgiveness for the USA's sins by the sacrifice of Jesus** *Why? To restore God's favor and to live in grace.*

Bible Blessings: How to Guarantee God Will Save the USA and Bless You

The curses from sin are removed by: (1) Atonement for our personal and national sins by Jesus Christ on the cross; and (2) Asking God to be forgiven. So the next Bible Truth has two parts: the cross brings back God's favor (atonement) and when we ask for forgiveness, then we live in God's grace.

The Seventh Bible Truth is restoring the cross and praying to receive forgiveness for the USA's sins by the sacrifice of Jesus will save the USA and bless your life. This is how we have favor and live in God's grace. Each of us and our nation are on the LORD's side when we believe that Jesus Christ's death on the cross forgives our sins.

Restoring the altar of the LORD is part of what King Asa did to end judgment (2 Chronicles 15:8). When God plagued Israel during King David's time, David built an altar to God and prayed and the plague ended (2 Samuel 24:25).

Even though our nation is guilty, God desires His mercy for us too. He wants to spare our Christian nation. What stops God from destroying us? He remembers our covenant through Jesus Christ who took God's wrath for our sins on the cross.

We must put our faith in our Lord dying on the cross for us to restore the altar today. Restoring the Cross brings Heaven on earth—for you personally and for the USA. Jesus Christ became a curse for us by hanging on the tree. By faith in Him, He makes us and the USA "white as snow" (Galatians 3:13, Isaiah 1:18). Remember, Calvary's tree is God's answer to the analogy of the bricks falling and the sycamore tree being cut down in *The Harbinger* book. Jesus Christ is the hope for America's future!

When Jesus forgave our sins on the cross, He was sealing and keeping covenant. His blood is the blood of the covenant. *The blood of Jesus Christ His Son cleanses us from all sin* (1 John 1:7). He *put away sin by the sacrifice of Himself* (Hebrews 9:26). Jesus paid the price that was required for our false gods, covetousness, courts betraying our founders by "ruling" their Christian ways are unconstitutional, and all sins. Without Jesus' blood, there is God's wrath and judgment.

The blood of Jesus is more powerful than any sin. The nail prints Jesus has from the three nails when they crucified Him proves that He loves us and paid the price for our sins.

The cross says there is forgiveness for all who believe in Him. To be forgiven, pray: *Father, I confess my sins of ___. I am cleansed by Jesus Christ's blood. In Jesus' name. Amen.*

Ask God to Forgive the USA

Do you feel sorrowful for our nation's sins, such as ministers turning to the world by saying its okay to vote for unbelievers and representatives ignoring life begins at conception and ending the life of one, two... and even seven or more pound babies by abortion? Our consciences are to convict us that it is shameful to not have Christianity in schools.

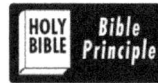

The church receives forgiveness for the USA.

The sins of our land stand out. God expects us to weep and wail over them (James 4:9). They will either be forgiven by Jesus Christ, or the USA will be punished.

Some say America has gone beyond the point of no return, but Jesus says no. As it is for your life, there is no need to look beyond our Good Shepherd because when we combine God and country together Jesus Christ is our Mediator.

The restoration of God's favor, by the cross and the blood of Jesus symbolized, ended the plague that killed 14,700 people because of the rebellion of Korah (Numbers 16:46-50). Then when the people of Israel grumbled God's judgment came, but whoever looked to the serpent of brass on the pole was healed (Numbers 21). The serpent on the pole represents Jesus who took our judgment on the cross. *As Moses lifted up the serpent in the wilderness, even so must the Son of man be lifted up (John 3:14).* There is atonement in Jesus Christ.

Moses prayed for God to pardon Israel's iniquities in the Old Covenant, but the USA's iniquities are forgiven because of Jesus. Paul assures us that even the chief of sinners can be forgiven. Even though some think the USA has transgressed beyond recovery, Jesus says, "forgive them". But we have to ask to be forgiven to end the curses from sin. There is hope!

By humbling themselves before God, Kings Asa and Josiah saw their nations healed. The Bible shows that Esther's actions saved Israel. God does deal with nations.

"What can wash away our sins? Nothing but the blood of Jesus." What can make the USA whole again? Nothing but the blood of Jesus. His blood cleanses us and removes the curses.

Americans owe our lives and the future of our nation to Jesus Christ. If you don't want to live in a nation under advanced judgment, then receive forgiveness by Jesus' blood for the USA playing the harlot with other gods, the military unashamedly defying God with gay sin, representatives disobeying God, shedding innocent blood, and all our sins. Instead of quenching the Holy Spirit by unrepented sins, the blood of Jesus cleanses us and brings the Holy Spirit.

Can our nation be forgiven if all don't seek to be forgiven? Yes. Jesus bore our sins. Not everyone in Israel believed God would give mercy when Moses asked God for it. Each person still must ask for their personal forgiveness by Jesus who was wounded for our transgressions and bruised for our iniquities (Isaiah 53:5). But the church receives forgiveness for our nation by faith (Exodus 32, Joel 2:17, Romans 4:5-7). We know God seeks for a man among them to make up the hedge and to stand in the gap before Him (Ezekiel 22:30). So I stand declaring the USA's sins are forgiven because of Jesus Christ.

Receive Forgiveness for the USA

The King who loves and forgives you is the same King who forgives our Christian nation. God's justice would have destroyed our nation already were it not for Jesus Christ taking the wrath of God on Himself to satisfy God's justice. Jesus says, "Forgive the USA" (1 John 1:7).

To restore jobs, have liberty, get out of debt, remove terrorism, have godly healthcare, protect our environment, and secure our borders, we must ask for forgiveness right now. Let's approach God with holy reverence and boldness, knowing that Jesus is the Lamb of God who takes away our sins. We have not transgressed beyond God's grace and mercy. It is amazing to think about the magnitude of God's love for us. Just as we believe and stay in covenant agreement that our sins are forgiven, we must do the same for the USA.

We cannot let anyone deny Jesus Christ's blood cleansing our sins, for He heals our lives and our land. Join me in thanking God. Then by faith ask God to forgive the USA.

Next, we will fully restore God's blessings.

✝ Prayer to Forgive the USA's Sins

Father,

You are merciful. With godly sorrow Americans ask for Your mercy for our sins instead of Your judgment. John 8:11, Jonah 4:2, Amos 5:18

The USA confesses and repents of:

- *Other gods Matthew 4:10*
- *Not having Christian religious liberty as our priority as a nation Mark 12:30*
- *Not following Jesus Christ in government, schools, courts and the military, and taking the Holy Bible & Christian prayer out of schools 2 Tim. 2:12, Is. 59:21*

127

- *Not demanding our God-given rights of life, liberty, the pursuit of happiness, property, and conscience* Genesis 1:27, Acts 5:29
- *Helping the wicked instead of supporting Christians in politics and business* 2 Timothy 3:5, 2 Chronicles 19:2, 2 Corinthians 6:14-18
- *Abortion* Matthew 5:17
- *Unjust wars* Mark 12:31
- *Coveting* Matthew 6:24, Ephesians 5:5
- *Homosexuality, adultery and fornication* Jude 7, 1 Corinthians 6:9-10
- *Occult, sorcery, and witchcraft* Deuteronomy 18:10-12
- *All other sins* 2 Chronicles 7:14

We receive forgiveness for our personal and national sins by the sacrifice of Jesus. 1 John 1:7 & 9

In Jesus' name. Amen.

✓ Summary and Reflection Questions

The restoration of God's favor (atonement) to us and our covenant Christian nation is by Jesus Christ. The cross removes sin's curse and ends God's judgment that we have seen. The Lamb of God is our hope and confidence. By asking God for forgiveness through Jesus Christ we are cleansed and forgiven (1 John 1:7, 9, Hebrews 9:26, Joel 4:2).

1. *What is the meaning of this verse, "the blood of Jesus Christ His Son cleanses us from all sin" (1 John 1:7)?*
2. *Explain why God is satisfied with the sacrifice of Jesus to give us the restoration of His favor.*
3. *Are you confident that Jesus bore your sins on the cross for you and you are forgiven? Why?*
4. *In what ways does asking God to forgive the USA's sins give you hope?*

10

First Truth Reprise—Covenant Blessings and Favor

"They entered into a covenant to seek the LORD
God of their fathers with all their heart and all their soul;"
2 Chronicles 15:12 KJV

We have learned that God has a plan for our nation, which is to give Him our hearts re-affirming: The LORD is the God of the USA and Americans are His people. Our *One Nation Under God* covenant relationship is what frees us from danger and protects our loved ones. He doesn't want to destroy the USA, but asks us to follow Him. We have much to thank Him for.

By learning the *7 Bible Truths*, we can now fully live out *the First Bible Truth*. We are going to seal our covenant, so prepare your heart before God because this is holy. As Jesus Christ purchased our salvation with His blood, He purchased the USA to be His covenant Christian nation. Because God gives Americans everything in covenant, will you let Him know that you submit yourself and the USA entirely to Him?

First Bible Truth Reprise
to end God's judgment
Psalm 33:12, 2 Cor. 6:16

Your re-affirming the USA's covenant with God is a holy act that says Americans are God's people

Why? To restore God's blessings and favor.

Bible Blessings: How to Guarantee God Will Save the USA and Bless You

Kings Asa and Josiah rejoiced to covenant with God when they recognized Judah was in judgment for their sin. Not everyone was in covenant and some resisted, but that didn't stop those with faith to follow God. And He rewarded the righteous who loved Him. Moses was faithful to God and kept covenant, so God blessed Israel.

HOLY BIBLE *Bible Principle*

Are you on the LORD's side? If so, then decide, "As for me and my house we will serve the LORD."

I thank God for you who agree that the USA is on the LORD's side by re-affirming our covenant. The strongest protection our nation has, with God's invincible national security, comes from consecrating the USA to God. Jesus Christ gave His blood to seal this covenant. In love we give our hearts to God to live for Him as our part.

Having a Christian government that serves the LORD as our Lawgiver, strong families with children protected, a nation that values our God-given rights, and hope are from covenant.

We who are in covenant live our lives for God and our sins are forgiven by God's great grace and mercy. God is good!

The *7 Bible Truths* presented in this book are shown in the following picture. These Bible promises are God's answer to end His judgment. The crisis threatening our nation's survival and our future will end. There is no other way to save our nation and to protect the next generations. Covenant gives us confidence the USA will be abundantly blessed again!

7 BIBLE TRUTHS THAT SAVE THE USA FROM DESTRUCTION

First Bible Truth *Psalm 33:12, 2 Cor. 6:18*	**Re-affirm Covenant: The LORD is the God of the USA and Americans are His people** *Why? To get the USA in right relationship with God.*
Second Bible Truth *2 Chron. 15:12, Matt. 7:7*	**Seek God with all your heart and all your soul** *Why? To find and be near to God.*
Third Bible Truth *Luke 6:47-49, 2 Chron. 34:31*	**Obey the Holy Bible with all your heart and all your soul** *Why? To do God's will.*
Fourth Bible Truth *Isaiah 33:22, Phil. 2:11*	**Have no king but King Jesus** *Why? Jesus brings the Kingdom of God's blessings of liberty, abundance, and peace.*
Fifth Bible Truth *Matt. 28:19-20, Is. 59:21*	**Make disciples of the USA** *Why? To raise godly generations.*
Sixth Bible Truth *2 Tim. 3:5, 2 Chron. 15:8*	**Turn away from everything against Jesus Christ** *Why? To love God.*
Seventh Bible Truth *1 John 1:7, Jonah 4:2*	**Restore the Cross and receive forgiveness for the USA's sins by the sacrifice of Jesus** *Why? To restore God's favor and to live in grace.*

†▬

The good news is Christians are in charge of the USA. We always will be. Healing comes for our nation by putting Jesus Christ and the Holy Bible first. American historian Benjamin Morris said, *The chief security and glory of the United States of America has been, is now, and will be forever, the prevalence and domination of the Christian Faith.*[1]

Unfortunately, we were taught to be politically correct and that false religions were to be present in our schools, military, and government. Then those outside of covenant worked to try to take our Christian faith away which led to these great judgments and even the danger of a final judgment. But we hold fast and say no! The LORD is the God of the USA!

We don't deserve such a covenant that heals our land by mercy and grace. Have you thought how important you are to God? Do you realize how much He cares for Americans?

God wants you to decide to give Him one of the greatest assets He has on earth: The USA as His covenant Christian nation. He says, *I will be their God, and they shall be My people* (2 Corinthians 6:16 KJV). Our founders taught that covenant applies to our Christian republic as we have seen.

Will You Join Covenant?

True Americans stand up for God even if others think differently. The Jamestown Settlers, Pilgrims, and others arrived to a godless land. They show us how a few people by faith can turn a heathen land to be the strongest Christian nation ever. Now, we who believe must work to make the USA the greatest Christian nation ever. Here are questions to ask yourself to see that you love God and country:

7 Questions to Seal the USA's Covenant with God

1. Do I publicly say: The LORD is the God of the USA and Americans are His people?
2. Am I seeking God with all my heart and all my soul, including for our nation?
3. Do I speak up for the USA to obey the Holy Bible?
4. Am I living with Jesus as King of the USA?
5. Will I help make disciples of our nation?
6. Do I speak up for our nation to turn away from everything against Jesus Christ?
7. Have I restored the cross and prayed to receive forgiveness for the USA's sins by Jesus' blood?

If you answer yes to these questions, you are on the LORD's side and He invites you to join covenant. You must agree to be in this covenant. Those not agreeing are outside of covenant. We know the only way to save the USA from the troubles that threaten our future is to re-affirm covenant, while receiving forgiveness for our country's sins through the sacrifice of Jesus. This is *God's Plan for the USA*. Jesus Christ is the only hope for our nation.

Our founders had faith for Americans to serve God. We must have faith! As you get ready to pray, thank the LORD that He is our God. Then examine yourself if there is any sin you can confess to God. When we seal covenant the devil's works are destroyed (1 John 3:8). Like our founders, we join God and country together forever. Americans love God!

✝ *Covenant Prayer*

To re-affirm covenant, pray and sign the following prayer. As an individual, family, or church, you may want to take communion as this is a holy covenant through Jesus Christ.

Save the USA from Destruction
Pray and Live: The USA's Covenant with God   ✝▦

Father,

You are holy. We thank You that the USA is dedicated to You in covenant to all generations.

LORD, You are the God of the USA and Americans are Your people. We seek You and obey the Holy Bible with all our heart and all our soul. As Jesus is our King, our nation makes Christian disciples and we turn away from everything against Jesus Christ.

We agree with You that the USA is to have marriage as one man and one woman only, have the Bible and Christian prayer in schools, and ban abortion again. We work and pray for covenant Christian leaders to immediately replace those disobeying You.

We thank You for the Cross and by Jesus' blood we receive forgiveness for the USA's sins. In Jesus' name. Amen.

_____
Your Name

For our safety and protection, we let God know that we agree with Him and not the Supreme Court's rebellious, anti-God opinions, including same-sex marriage, removing our founder's Christianity from schools, abortion, and separation of church and state. These great sins, along with false gods and voting for unbelievers, have caused most of the troubles and dangers to our nation and families.

Print and put *The USA's Covenant with God* on your refrigerator, by your desk, and inside your church or ministry's bulletins to re-affirm it often. You can also take a picture of it to save and share it. On the second Sunday of each month, join our nation in praying our covenant so the USA is guaranteed to have God's blessings and not His judgment. At my website, www.USA.church, there are many free resources to use in your home, church, work, and school.

Now, let's live the American Dream *to advance the Kingdom of our Lord Jesus Christ and to enjoy the liberties of the Gospel in purity and peace.*[2] How will all generations of our beloved nation know how to glorify God unless we teach them to have hearts like Jesus? What will you do to make these *7 Bible Truths* part of your daily life?

✓ Summary and Reflection Questions

We walk close with God by covenant and living in covenant guarantees that He will give you and our nation liberty, abundance, and peace. His rich blessings are seen when the USA exalts Jesus Christ and honors Christians.

1. *Are you in covenant? Have you agreed with the 7 Bible Truths?*
2. *Why does our nation following Jesus give you hope?*
3. *The next step of God's Plan for the USA is to ask others to re-affirm covenant. Who can you and your church invite to join covenant? How?*

৩৯

Thank you for reading "God's Plan for the USA". I thank God for you and I pray for you daily. Your love for God and country gives me great joy. To save the USA and make our nation great again, you and your church are invited to use the many free resources at USA Christian Church. Let's unite the USA in Christ by working together. You can also sign up for my daily email and social media.

Jesus Christ is the hope for your and America's future! Pray how you can help share:

- ***"God's Plan for the USA"***
- ***The 7 Bible Truths***

And I invite you and your church to join:

- ***One Million Americans on the LORD's Side**[TM] USA.church*
- ***The American Disciple Making Team**[TM] page 102*
- ***The Daily Biblical Prayer for Government**[TM] page 100*
- ***Wednesdays: Nationwide Prayer and Fasting**[TM] page 100*
- ***Christians Uniting to Save the USA**[TM] page 101*

Always remember, Jesus loves you!

Rev. Steven Andrew
USA Christian Church
www.USA.church

The Declaration of Independence

"The Declaration of Independence laid the cornerstone of human government upon the first precepts of Christianity." John Quincy Adams

There is a place to sign at the end.

In CONGRESS July 4, 1776.

The unanimous Declaration of the thirteen united States of America,

When in the course of human events, it becomes necessary for one people to dissolve the political bands which have connected them with another, and to assume among the powers of the earth, the separate and equal station to which the laws of nature and of nature's God entitle them, a decent respect to the opinions of mankind requires that they should declare the causes which impel them to the separation.

We hold these truths to be self-evident:

That all men are created equal; that they are endowed by their Creator with certain unalienable rights; that among these are life, liberty, and the pursuit of happiness; that, to secure these rights, governments are instituted among men, deriving their just powers from the consent of the governed; that whenever any form of government becomes destructive of these ends, it is the right of the people to alter or to abolish it, and to institute new government, laying its foundation on such principles, and organizing its powers in such form, as to them shall seem most likely to effect their safety and happiness. Prudence, indeed, will dictate that governments long established should not be changed for light and transient causes; and accordingly all experience hath shown that mankind are more disposed to suffer, while evils are sufferable than to right themselves by abolishing the forms to which they are accustomed. But when a long train of abuses and usurpations, pursuing invariably the same object, evinces a design to reduce them under absolute despotism, it is their right, it is their duty, to throw off such government, and to provide new guards for their future security.

Such has been the patient sufferance of these colonies; and such is now the necessity which constrains them to alter their former systems of government. The history of the present King of Great Britain is a history of repeated injuries and usurpations, all having in direct object the establishment of an absolute tyranny over these states. To prove this, let facts be submitted to a candid world.

He has refused his assent to laws, the most wholesome and necessary for the public good.

He has forbidden his governors to pass laws of immediate and pressing importance, unless suspended in their operation till his assent should be obtained; and, when so suspended, he has utterly neglected to attend to them.

He has refused to pass other laws for the accommodation of large districts of people, unless those people would relinquish the right of representation in the legislature, a right inestimable to them, and formidable to tyrants only.

He has called together legislative bodies at places unusual uncomfortable, and distant from the depository of their public records, for the sole purpose of fatiguing them into compliance with his measures.

He has dissolved representative houses repeatedly, for opposing, with manly firmness, his invasions on the rights of the people.

He has refused for a long time, after such dissolutions, to cause others to be elected; whereby the legislative powers, incapable of annihilation, have returned to the people at large for their exercise; the state remaining, in the mean time, exposed to all the dangers of invasions from without and convulsions within.

He has endeavored to prevent the population of these states; for that purpose obstructing the laws for naturalization of foreigners; refusing to pass others to encourage their migration hither, and raising the conditions of new appropriations of lands.

He has obstructed the administration of justice, by refusing his assent to laws for establishing judiciary powers.

He has made judges dependent on his will alone, for the tenure of their offices, and the amount and payment of their salaries.

He has erected a multitude of new offices, and sent hither swarms of officers to harass our people and eat out their substance.

He has kept among us, in times of peace, standing armies, without the consent of our legislatures.

He has affected to render the military independent of, and superior to, the civil power.

He has combined with others to subject us to a jurisdiction foreign to our Constitution and unacknowledged by our laws, giving his assent to their acts of pretended legislation:

For quartering large bodies of armed troops among us;

For protecting them, by a mock trial, from punishment for any murders which they should commit on the inhabitants of these states;

For cutting off our trade with all parts of the world;

For imposing taxes on us without our consent;

For depriving us, in many cases, of the benefits of trial by jury;

For transporting us beyond seas, to be tried for pretended offenses;

For abolishing the free system of English laws in a neighboring province, establishing therein an arbitrary government, and enlarging its boundaries, so as to render it at once an example and fit instrument for introducing the same absolute rule into these colonies;

For taking away our charters, abolishing our most valuable laws, and altering fundamentally the forms of our governments;

For suspending our own legislatures, and declaring themselves invested with power to legislate for us in all cases whatsoever.

He has abdicated government here, by declaring us out of his protection and waging war against us.

He has plundered our seas, ravaged our coasts, burned our towns, and destroyed the lives of our people.

He is at this time transporting large armies of foreign mercenaries to complete the works of death, desolation, and tyranny already begun with circumstances of cruelty and perfidy scarcely paralleled in the most barbarous ages, and totally unworthy the head of a civilized nation.

He has constrained our fellow-citizens, taken captive on the high seas, to bear arms against their country, to become the executioners of their friends and brethren, or to fall themselves by their hands.

He has excited domestic insurrection among us, and has endeavored to bring on the inhabitants of our frontiers the merciless Indian savages, whose known rule of warfare is an undistinguished destruction of all ages, sexes, and conditions.

In every stage of these oppressions we have petitioned for redress in the most humble terms; our repeated petitions have been answered only by repeated injury. A prince, whose character is thus marked by every act which may define a tyrant, is unfit to be the ruler of a free people.

Nor have we been wanting in our attentions to our British brethren. We have warned them, from time to time, of attempts by their legislature to extend an unwarrantable jurisdiction over us. We have reminded them of the circumstances of our emigration and settlement here. We have appealed to their native justice and magnanimity; and we have conjured them, by the ties of our common kindred, to disavow these usurpations which would inevitably interrupt our connections and correspondence. They too, have been deaf to the voice of justice and of consanguinity. We must, therefore, acquiesce in the necessity which denounces our separation, and hold them as we hold the rest of mankind, enemies in war, in peace friends.

We, therefore, the representatives of the United States of America, in General Congress assembled, appealing to the Supreme Judge of the world for the rectitude of our intentions, do, in the name and by the authority of the good people of these colonies solemnly publish and declare, That these United Colonies are, and of right ought to be, FREE AND INDEPENDENT STATES; that they are absolved from all allegiance to the British crown and that all political connection between them and the state of Great Britain is, and ought to be, totally dissolved; and that, as free and independent states, they have full power to levy war, conclude peace, contract alliances, establish commerce, and do all other acts and things which independent states may of right do. And for the support of this declaration, with a firm reliance on the protection of Divine Providence, we mutually pledge to each other our lives, our fortunes, and our sacred honor.

[Signed by] JOHN HANCOCK [President]

New Hampshire
JOSIAH BARTLETT,
WM. WHIPPLE,
MATTHEW THORNTON.

Massachusetts Bay
SAML. ADAMS,
JOHN ADAMS,
ROBT.TREAT PAINE,
ELBRIDGE GERRY.

Rhode Island
STEP. HOPKINS,
WILLIAM ELLERY.

Connecticut
ROGER SHERMAN,
SAM'EL
    HUNTINGTON,
WM. WILLIAMS,
OLIVER WOLCOTT.

New York
WM. FLOYD,
PHIL. LIVINGSTON,
FRANS. LEWIS,
LEWIS MORRIS.

New Jersey
RICHD. STOCKTON,
JNO.WITHERSPOON,
FRAS. HOPKINSON,
JOHN HART,
ABRA. CLARK.

Pennsylvania
ROBT. MORRIS
BENJAMIN RUSH,
BENJA. FRANKLIN,
JOHN MORTON,
GEO. CLYMER,
JAS. SMITH,
GEO. TAYLOR,
JAMES WILSON,
GEO. ROSS.

Delaware
CAESAR RODNEY,
GEO. READ,
THO. M'KEAN.

Maryland
JAMES WILSON,
SAMUEL CHASE,
WM. PACA,
THOS. STONE,
CHARLES CARROLL of
    Carrollton.

Virginia
GEORGE WYTHE,
RICHARD HENRY LEE,
TH. JEFFERSON,
BENJA. HARRISON,
THS. NELSON, JR.,
FRANCIS LIGHTFOOT
    LEE,
CARTER BRAXTON.

North Carolina
WM. HOOPER,
JOSEPH HEWES,
JOHN PENN.

South Carolina
EDWARD RUTLEDGE,
THOS. HAYWARD,
    JUNR.,
THOMAS LYNCH,
    JUNR.,
ARTHUR MIDDLETON.

Georgia
BUTTON GWINNETT,
LYMAN HALL,
GEO.WALTON.

---

* Sign Here

REFERENCES

Introduction: The Crisis That Threatens the USA's Survival ... And Our Future

[1] "Mike Huckabee blasts same-sex marriage ruling," foxnews.com, June 29, 2015, (video from 2:25 to 8:02) http://www.foxnews.com/transcript/2015/06/29/mike-huckabee-blasts-same-sex-marriage-ruling

[2] "Mike Huckabee: We Must Stand with Kim Davis Against 'Criminalization of Christianity', breitbart.com, September 7, 2015, http://bit.ly/1Lfftkm

[3] "Same-Sex Marriage Ruling Is Another Roe v. Wade," beitbart.com, June 26, 2015, http://dailysignal.com/2015/07/02/state-silences-bakers-who-refused-to-make-cake-for-lesbian-couple-fines-them-135k

[4] "Same-sex Marriage Is Not Law, Says Mike Huckabee," usa.church, November 14, 2015, https://www.usa.church/2015/11/14/same-sex-marriage-is-not-law-says-mike-huckabee/

[5] "DHS Caught Busing in Illegal Somalis from Mexican Border," wnd.com, May 13, 2015, http://bit.ly/1Ng5o7p

[6] "For Many American States, It's Like the Recession Never Ended," bloomberg.com, accessed May 20, 2015, http://www.bloomberg.com/news/articles/2015-05-20/six-years-into-recovery-u-s-states-struggle-to-balance-budgets

[7] "40 percent of unemployed have quit looking for jobs," cnbc.com, accessed May 20, 2015, http://www.cnbc.com/id/102694868

[8] "Feds Spent $100 Billion on Food Assistance Last Year," freebeacon.com, accessed May 20, 2015, http://freebeacon.com/issues/feds-spent-100-billion-on-food-assistance-last-year/

[9] "Yuan to supersede dollar as top reserve currency: Survey," cnbc.com, February 26, 2014, http://www.cnbc.com/id/101450365

[10] "Who's your debt daddy? China tops list of US foreign creditors once more," cnbc.com, May 16, 2015, http://www.cnbc.com/id/102684920

[11] "U.S. Achievement Stalls as Other Nations Make Gains," edweek.com, Dec. 3, 2013, http://www.edweek.org/ew/articles/2013/12/03/14pisa.h33.html

[12] "DHS to Purchase 62 Million More Rounds of AR-15 Ammo," infowars.com, April 15, 2015, http://bit.ly/1OCvqor

[13] Noah Webster, History of the United States, (New-Haven..., 1832), 326-327

[14] "U.S. and Chinese troops connect in first-ever exchange at JBLM," thenewstribune.com, Nov. 20, 2015, http://bit.ly/1Sc8jSV

[15] "German Air Force... to move to Holloman Air Force Base in New Mexico," nbcdfw.com, Mar. 11, 2013, http://bit.ly/1TkpTVK

1 Do You Want the USA to Follow God?

[1] The full covenant prayer is in Chapter 3 on page 41

[2] Abraham Lincoln, Presidential Proclamation, (March 30, 1863)

[3] Yale Law School, "The Articles of Confederation of the United Colonies of New England; May 19, 1643," *avalon.law.yale.edu*, accessed January 12, 2015, http://avalon.law.yale.edu/17th_century/art1613.asp

[4] John Hancock, Massachusetts Governor's Proclamation, (October 15, 1791)

[5] Gallup CEO Jim Clifton Interview on Fox News, *youtube.com*, February 5, 2015, https://www.youtube.com/watch?v=CTRAibMiLZ8

[6] "It's official: America is now No. 2," *marketwatch.com*, December 4, 2014, http://www.marketwatch.com/story/its-official-america-is-now-no-2-2014-12-04, and "Does size matter? China poised to overtake US as world's largest economy in 2014," *ft.com*, April 30, 2014, http://blogs.ft.com/the-world/2014/04/does-size-matter-china-poised-to-overtake-us-as-worlds-largest-economy-in-2014/

[7] Library of Congress, "Religion and the Founding of the American Republic," accessed January 12, 2015, *loc.gov*, http://www.loc.gov/exhibits/religion/rel04.html

[8] Charles Francis Adams, The Works of John Adams, Second President..., Volume 3, (Boston, Charles C. Little and James Brown, 1851), 241

[9] Charles Francis Adams, The Works of John Adams, Second President..., Volume 9, (Boston, Charles C. Little and James Brown, 1854), 169

[10] John Winthrop, A Model of Christian Charity, (1630)

[11] The New York Sabbath Committee, First Five Years of the Sabbath Reform, 1857-62, (New York, Edward O. Jenkins, Printer, 1862), 43

[12] Abraham Lincoln, Presidential Proclamation, (March 30, 1863)

[13] Noah Webster, Letters to a Young Gentleman Commencing His Education..., (New Haven, Howe and Spalding, 1823), 7

[14] George Washington, Presidential Proclamation, (October 3, 1789)

[15] Abraham Lincoln, Presidential Proclamation, (March 30, 1863)

2 Signs and Wonders of Judgment

[1] Office of the Management and Budget, "Mid Session Review, Budget of the U.S. Government," *gpo.gov*, accessed January 12, 2015, http://www.gpo.gov/fdsys/pkg/BUDGET-2015-MSR/pdf/BUDGET-2015-MSR.pdf, 74

[2] "Greek Prime Minister Calls Bank Workers' Riot Deaths 'Murder'," foxnew.com, May, 5, 2010, http://www.foxnews.com/world/2010/05/05/brigade-says-person-dead-bank-riots-demonstration/

[3] "High Taxes, Abusive Enforcement Causing Businesses, Citizens to Flee America," *breitbart.com*, accessed January 12, 2015, http://bit.ly/1qX64te

[4] "Exclusive: Signs of Declining Economic Security," *bigstory.ap.org*, accessed January 12, 2015, http://bigstory.ap.org/article/exclusive-4-5-us-face-near-poverty-no-work-0

[5] "It's official: America is now No. 2," *marketwatch.com*, Dec. 4, 2014, http://www.marketwatch.com/story/its-official-america-is-now-no-2-2014-12-04, and "Does size matter? China poised to overtake US as world's largest economy in 2014," *ft.com*, April 30, 2014, http://blogs.ft.com/the-world/2014/04/does-size-matter-china-poised-to-overtake-us-as-worlds-largest-economy-in-2014/

[6] "Congressional Performance," *rasmussenreports.com,* Dec. 26, 2014, http://www. rasmussenreports.com/public_content/politics/top_stories/congressional_performance

[7] "Obama Faces Congressional Backlash for Supporting Al Qaeda Syria Rebels," *infowars.com,* July 1, 2013, http://www.infowars.com/obama-faces-congressional-backlash-for-supporting-al-qaeda-syria-rebels/, "DHS Gave Muslim Brotherhood VIP Treatment, No TSA Pat Downs," *infowars.com,* January 20, 2014, http://www.infowars.com/dhs-gave-muslim-brotherhood-vip-treatment-no-tsa-pat-downs/, "Atheists meet with White House officials," *usatoday.com,* Feb. 26, 2010, http://content.usatoday.com/communities/Religion/post/2010/02/atheists-meet-with-white-house-officials

[8] "Obama Omits Creator-in Declaration of Independence," usanewsfirst.com, July 5, 2012, http://www.usanewsfirst.com/2012/07/05/obama-omits-creator-in-declaration-of-independence

[9] "Obamacare Architect: Yeah, We Lied to The 'Stupid' American People to Get It Passed," townhall.com, November 10, 2014, http://townhall.com/tipsheet/katiepavlich/2014/11/10/obamacare-architect-yeah-we-lied-to-the-stupid-american-people-n1916605

[10] "5 Lies the Democrats Told To Sell Obamacare," townhall.com, June 4, 2013, http://townhall.com/columnists/johnhawkins/2013/06/04/5-lies-the-democrats-told-to-sell-obamacare-n1612356/page/full

[11] "ObamaCare 'death panel' faces growing opposition from Democrats," thehill.com, August, 8, 2013, http://thehill.com/policy/healthcare/316045-obamacare-cost-cutting-board-faces-growing-opposition-from-democrats, "Sarah Palin Right All Along? Howard Dean's Surprising ObamaCare Claim," foxnew.com, July 30, 2013, http://insider.foxnews.com/2013/07/30/howard-dean-op-ed-supports-sarah-palins-obamacare-death-panels-claim

[12] "Obamacare offers firms $3,000 incentive to hire illegals over native-born workers," washingtontimes.com, November 24, 2014, http://www.washingtontimes.com/news/2014/nov/25/obama-amnesty-obamacare-clash-businesses-have-3000/

[13] "Fewer US-Born Americans Have Jobs Now Than In 2007," dailycaller.com, December, 19, 2014, http://dailycaller.com/2014/12/19/fewer-us-born-americans-have-jobs-now-than-in-2007/

[14] "Kids wear red, white and blue in spite of no America Day", jhnewsandguide.com, October 1, 2015, http://www.jhnewsandguide.com/news/schools/kids-wear-red-white-and-blue-in-spite-of-no/article_887a4633-8d20-55ba-afbf-8130d199867c.html

[15] "Judicial Watch: New Documents Show Homeland Security Released...," *judicialwatch.org,* March 23, 2015, http://bit.ly/1FTRpnM

[16] "Father of son killed by illegal alien has message for Obama," foxnews.com, May, 5, 2010, http://video.foxnews.com/v/3900984098001/father-of-son-killed-by-illegal-alien-has-message-for-obama/

[17] "BREAKING: Pier 14 Murder Suspect Had Been Deported 5 Times with 7 Felonies", breitbart.com, July 3, 2015,

http://www.breitbart.com/texas/2015/07/03/breaking-pier-14-murder-suspect-had-been-deported-5-times-with-7-felonies/

[18] "Homeland Security: Fundamentalists Possible Terrorists – Anti-God Obama After Christians," *usanewsfirst.com,* July 8, 2012, http://www.usanewsfirst.com/2012/07/08/homeland-security-anti-abortion-groups-possible-terrorists-anti-god-obama-after-christians

[19] "Jeh Johnsons malfeasance," *washingtontimes.com,* March 26, 2015, http://bit.ly/1xjcjuX

[20] "NSA Spies on Americans Through Your TV with FLAME Spy Program," *usanewsfirst.com,* August 6, 2013, http://www.usanewsfirst.com/2013/08/06/nsa-spies-on-americans-through-your-tv-with-flame-spy-program/

[21] "Justice Department Spies on Millions of Cars: WSJ," *msn.com,* January 27, 2015, http://bit.ly/1IAYBF1

[22] "Can We End Christian Persecution?," *usanewsfirst.com,* accessed July 17, 2015, http://bit.ly/1bLgVR5

[23] "Christians Outraged Obama Removed USA Military Cross in Afghanistan," *usanewsfirst.com,* January 25, 2013, http://bit.ly/1Bt4r5A

3 First Truth: America's 7 Secret: Choose the True God

[1] John Witherspoon, The Works of the Reverend John Witherspoon Vol. III, (Philadelphia, William W. Woodward, 1802), 42

[2] Benjamin Franklin Morris, Christian Life and Character of the Civil Institutions of the United States..., (Cincinnati, George W. Childs, 1864), 337

[3] Yale Law School, "The Articles of Confederation of the United Colonies of New England; May 19, 1643," *avalon.law.yale.edu,* accessed January 12, 2015, http://avalon.law.yale.edu/17th_century/art1613.asp

[4] R. S. Thomas, The Religious Element in the Settlement at Jamestown, (The Sixth Annual Council of the Diocese of Southern Virginia, 1898) 3, 9

[5] Ibid., 36

[6] Dr. Paul Jehle, Plymouth Rock Foundation, "July 2012 E News," *plymrock.org,* July, 2012, http://www.plymrock.org/july2012news.php

[7] The Pilgrims, Mayflower Compact, (November 11, 1620)

[8] John Winthrop, A Model of Christian Charity, (1630)

[9] Alexander Biddle, Old Family Letters: Copied from the Originals, (Philadelphia, J. P. Lippincott Company, 1892), 248-249

[10] Library of Congress, "Religion and the Founding of the American Republic," acc. January 12, 2015, *loc.gov,* http://www.loc.gov/exhibits/religion/rel04.html

[11] John C. Fitzpatrick, The Writings of George Washington from the Original Manuscript Sources 1745-1799 Volume 15 May 6, 1779-July 28, 1779, (Library of Congress, 1939), 55

[12] Supreme Court, Church of the Holy Trinity v. United States, (Feb. 29, 1892)

[13] "11% of All Christians in the world Live in the USA," *usanewsfirst.com,* June 19, 2015, http://www.usanewsfirst.com/2015/06/13/11-of-all-christians-live-in-the-usa

[14] "Christians Greatly Outnumber All Others in the USA," *usanewsfirst.com*, June 13, 2015, http://bit.ly/1ebf5KS

[15] John Whiting and Henry Whiting, Revolutionary Orders of General Washington: Issued During the Years 1778, '80, '81, & '82 (New York and London, Wiley and Putnam, 1844) 32

[16] Benjamin Franklin Morris, Christian Life and Character of the Civil Institutions of the United States..., (Cincinnati, George W. Childs, 1864), 557

[17] Amos Blanchard, American Military and Naval Biography: Containing... the Officers of the Revolution, (Cincinnati, A. Salisbury, 1832), 476

[18] Sir William Blackstone, Commentaries on the Laws of England: In Four Books... Volume 1, (New York, W. E. Dean, 1838), 94

[19] Sir William Blackstone, Commentaries on the Laws of England: In the Order, and Compiled from... (London, Saunders and Benning, 1840), 20

[20] The Law Journal for 1806; Consisting of Original Communications..., (London, W. Clarke and Sons, 1807), 106

[21] Samuel Adams, The Writings of Samuel Adams: 1770-1773, (New York, G. P. Putnam's Sons, 1906), 355

[22] Benjamin Franklin Morris, Christian Life and Character of the Civil Institutions of the United States..., (Cincinnati, George W. Childs, 1864), 337

[23] Joseph Story, Commentaries on the Constitution of the United States: With a ..., Volume 3, (Boston, Hilliard, Gray, and Company, 1833), 728

[24] John Torrey Morse, American Statesmen: John Marshall Vol. X, (Boston and New York, Houghton, Mifflin and Company, 1899), 253

[25] John Profatt, The American Decisions: Cases of General Value and Authority Volume 1, (San Francisco, Bancroft-Whitney Co., 1910), 417

[26] Noah Webster, History of the United States, (New-Haven..., 1832), 299-300

[27] Library of Congress, "Religion and the Founding of the American Republic," acc. March 2, 2015, *loc.gov*, http://www.loc.gov/exhibits/religion/rel06-2.html

[28] William Vincent Wells, The Life and Public Services of Samuel Adams..., Vol. 2, (Boston, Little, Brown and Co., 1865), 223

4 Second Truth: Seek... Find

[1] George Washington, Presidential Proclamation, (October 3, 1789)

[2] "Praying to the LORD Only Brings Blessings," *God.news*, November 8, 2015, http://God.news/2015/11/08/praying-to-the-lord-only-brings-blessings/

[3] Robert Baird, Religion of the United States of America, (Glasgow and Edinburgh, Blackie and Son, 1844), 263, and Journals of the American Congress...1774-1788, Vol. I, (Washington: Way and Gideon, 1823), 309-310

[4] Benjamin Franklin Morris, Christian Life and Character of the Civil Institutions of the United States..., (Cincinnati, George W. Childs, 1864), 328, and Reports of Committees of the House of Representatives Made During the First Session..., (Washington: A. O. P. Nicholson, 1854)

[5] See Chapter 7 for details on Wednesdays: Nationwide Prayer and Fasting™

5 Third Truth: Living the Bible Way

[1] Sir William Blackstone, Commentaries on the Laws of England: In Four Books..., (Philadelphia, J.B. Lippincott & Co., 1859), Page 28

[2] W. C. Anderson, Review of Dr. Scott's Bible and Politics in the Light of Religion and the Law, (San Francisco, Towne and Bacon, 1858), 75

[3] James Wilson, The Works of the Honourable James Wilson... Vol. 1, (Philadelphia, Lorenzo Press,1804), 104-105

[4] "Christian Voting Guide," usa.church, accessed July 17, 2015, http://www.usa.church/christian-voting-guide/

[5] Williams Jay, The Life of John Jay: With Selections from His Correspondence and ..., Volume 2, (New York, J. & J. Harper, 1833), 376

[6] Noah Webster, History of the United States, (New-Haven..., 1832), 336-337

[7] Noah Webster, Letters to a Young Gentleman Commencing His Education..., (New Haven, Howe and Spalding, 1823), 18-19

[8] Williams Jay, The Life of John Jay: With Selections from His Correspondence and ..., Volume 2, (New York, J. & J. Harper, 1833), 351

[9] Abraham Lincoln, Complete Works Comprising his Speeches, Letters, State Papers, and Miscellaneous Writings Vol. Two, John Nicolay and John Hay, (New York: The Century Co., 1894), 574

[10] American Missionary Society, The American Missionary, Volume 20, (January 1876), 183

6 Fourth Truth: Jesus Rules the Nation

[1] Elizabeth Cooper, Popular History of America..., (London: Longman, Green, Longman, Roberts, & Green, 1865), 399

[2] George Washington, Presidential Proclamation, (October 3, 1789)

[3] Junius Brutus, A Defense of Liberty Against Tyrants, nlnrac.org, (1579, English Richard Baldwin 1689, accessed January 23, 2015),http://www.nlnrac.org/classical/late-medieval-transformations/documents/defense

[4] Jonathan Mayhew, A Discourse Concerning Unlimited Submission and Non-resistance to the Higher Powers, (1750), 25

7 Fifth Truth: Hearts to Be Like Jesus

[1] Abraham Lincoln, Presidential Proclamation, (March 30, 1863)

[2] Supreme Court, Church of the Holy Trinity v. United States, (Feb. 29, 1892)

[3] "Noah Webster," webstersdictionary1828.com, Accessed January 24, 2015, http://webstersdictionary1828.com/NoahWebster

[4] John C. Fitzpatrick, The Writings of George Washington from the Original Manuscript Sources 1745-1799, Vol. 15, (Library of Congress, 1939), 55

[5] W. C. Anderson, Review of Dr. Scott's Bible and Politics in the Light of Religion and the Law, (San Francisco, Towne and Bacon, 1858), 75

[6] American Missionary Society, The American Missionary, Vol. 20, (January 1876), 183

[7] William Vincent Wells, The Life and Public Services of Samuel Adams..., Vol. 2, (Boston, Little, Brown and Co., 1865), 223

8 Sixth Truth: Victory Over Sin

[1] "Christian Voting Guide," usa.church, accessed December 19, 2015, https://www.usa.church/christian-voters-guide/

[2] "Donald Trump Meets with Religious Leaders, Including Robert Jeffress," youtube.com, Sep. 30, 2015, https://www.youtube.com/watch?v=Uk4c2uoOF3o

[3] "Mormon founder Joseph Smith had as many as 40 wives," *news.yahoo.com,* November 11, 2014, http://news.yahoo.com/mormon-founder-joseph-smith-had-many-40-wives-212016652.html

[4] "Bible: Obama Damages to USA Increased as God's Judgment," usanewsfirst.com, acc. July 12, 2015, http://www.usanewsfirst.com/2014/12/28/bible-obama-damages-to-usa-increased-as-gods-judgment

[5] "Where Are the Christian Leaders? Pastors & the Mormon Cult," usanewsfirst.com, acc. Dec. 19, 2015, http://www.usanewsfirst.com/2014/12/16/where-are-the-christian-leaders-pastors-the-mormon-cult

[6] "Who's On the LORD's Side," usa.church, acc. December 19, 2015, https://www.usa.church/whos-on-the-lords-side/

[7] "99.8% of 2012 Voters Betrayed Jesus Christ," *usanewsfirst.com,* accessed July 12, 2015, http://bit.ly/1NwnQJJ

[8] "GAO Confirms... Abortion Advocates Spent About $1.5 Billion in Tax Dollars," *cnsnews.com,* March 26, 2015, http://bit.ly/1ODgTdg

[9] John Whiting and Henry Whiting, Revolutionary Orders of General Washington: Issued During the Years 1778, '80, '81, & '82 (New York and London, Wiley and Putnam, 1844) 75

[10] Ibid., 32

[11] William and Robert Chambers, Chamber's miscellany of instructive & entertaining tracts, Vol. 4 (Philadelphia, J. B. Lippincott & CO., 1858), 25

[12] "Prevalence and Awareness of HIV Infection Among Men Who Have Sex With Men..." cdc.gov, September 24, 2010, http://www.cdc.gov/mmwr/preview/mmwrhtml/mm5937a2.htm

[13] "New Study Shows Homosexuals Live 20 Fewer Years," *freerepublic.com,* June 6, 2005, http://www.freerepublic.com/focus/news/1417935/posts

[14] "Mike Huckabee blasts same-sex marriage ruling," foxnews.com, June 29, 2015, http://www.foxnews.com/transcript/2015/06/29/mike-huckabee-blasts-same-sex-marriage-ruling

9 Seventh Truth: God's Mercy and Forgiveness

[1] Abraham Lincoln, Presidential Proclamation, (March 30, 1863)

10 First Truth Reprise: Covenant Blessings and Favor

[1] Benjamin Franklin Morris, Christian Life and Character of the Civil Institutions of the United States..., (Cincinnati, George W. Childs, 1864), 11

[2] Yale Law School, "The Articles of Confederation of the United Colonies of New England; May 19, 1643," *avalon.law.yale.edu,* accessed January 12, 2015, http://avalon.law.yale.edu/17th_century/art1613.asp

Prayer of Salvation

Father,

Jesus Christ died to forgive my sins. I confess with my mouth the Lord Jesus. I believe in my heart that You raised Jesus from the dead. I ask You for the Holy Spirit. In Jesus' name. Amen. John 3:16, Romans 10:9-10

If you prayed to be a Christian, let me know at USA Christian Church at www.USA.church

Books By Pastor Steven Andrew

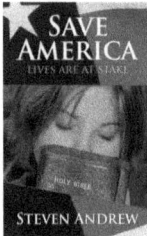

Save America

Paperback: ISBN 9780977955084
eBook: ISBN 9780977955046

Enhanced update of God's Plan for the USA

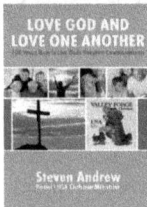

Love God and Love One Another

Paperback: ISBN 9780977955039
eBook: ISBN 9780977955084

Making A Strong Christian Nation

Paperback: ISBN 9780977955077

Check for these upcoming new books.

Are You an American?

The American Disciple Making Team™ Handbook

Government Serves God
Separation of Church and State is a Dangerous Lie

148